easy

HANGING
BASKETS
& WINDOW BOXES

COLLINS

easy

HANGING BASKETS
& WINDOW BOXES

Richard Jackson
&
Carolyn Hutchinson

HarperCollins*Publishers*

Acknowledgements

The publishers thank the following for their kind permission to reproduce the photographs in this book:

Garden Picture Library 5 (middle), 6, 53, 54, 64, 68 (Lynne Brotchie); 103 (right) (Linda Burgess); 70, 82 (top), 108, 110 (Brian Carter); 12 (bottom), 69 (middle), 77, 88 (left), 93 (left) (John Glover); 89 (bottom) (Sunniva Harte); 9 (Neil Holmes); 52, 55 (bottom), 75 (bottom), 83 (top) (Lamontagne); 44 (Jerry Pavia); 55 (top) (Howard Rice); 76 (left) (Stephen Robson); 10 (Friedrich Strauss); 37 (bottom), 39 (top) (Juliette Wade); **Gillian Beckett** 91 (top and bottom), 93 (right), 94 (top); **Colegrave Seeds** 21 (top), 37 (top), 38 (left and right), 45, 48 (top), 51 (bottom left), 78, 79 (top, middle and bottom), 80, 81 (top and bottom), 85 (bottom left), 86 (top), 87 (top and bottom), 88 (right), 103 (left), 104 (top and bottom); **Garden Innovations** 12 (top); **John Glover** 8, 14 (top and bottom), 20 (top), 42 (bottom), 43 (bottom), 46, 47, 58, 59, 65, 66, 67 (bottom), 69 (top), 90 (top and bottom), 92 (top and bottom), 94 (top), 96 (left), 99 (top); **Foxmoor Flower Tower Co Ltd/ Amalgamated Products Direct Ltd** 41 (centre); **Holt Studios** (Nigel Cattlin) 106, 109; **Hozelock Ltd** 20 (bottom); **Natural Image** (Bob Gibbons) 42 (top), 89 (top left), 95, 97; **Graham Strong** 16, 60, 61, 67; **Suttons Seeds** 11, 51 (top), 85 (top), 86 (bottom), 98 (top), 99 (bottom), 101 (bottom); **Textice Ltd** 23 (bottom right), 34-5; **Thompson & Morgan (UK) Ltd** 13 (bottom), 40 (left and right), 41 (left and right), 49 (top), 74, 75 (top), 83 (top); **Unwins Seeds Ltd** 39 (bottom), 48 (top), 50, 69 (bottom), 72, 73, 76 (right), 82 (bottom), 84 (top), 89 (top right), 96 (right), 98 (bottom), 100 (top and bottom), 101 (top).

Special thanks to Brian Smith of Woodlea Nurseries who helped with the planting sequences on pages 24-33.

All other photographs supplied by *Garden Answers* magazine.

First published in hardback in 1998 by HarperCollins*Publishers*, London
This paperback edition first published in 1999

A CIP catalogue record for this book is available from the British Library

ISBN 000 414057 5

Colour reproduction by Colourscan, Singapore
Printed and bound in Italy by Rotolito Lombarda, SpA, Milan

Contents

Introduction

This book provides everything you need to know to create and grow beautiful hanging baskets and window boxes. The ideas are easy to follow and the authors' expert tips and practical advice will inspire gardeners of all levels to have a go.

Collins Easy Hanging Baskets and Window Boxes *covers every kind of plant you can grow in a container, including flowers, fruit and vegetables, allowing gardeners to make full use of every inch of their garden – whatever its size. There are buying tips for baskets, boxes and plants plus solutions to everyday worries, such as watering and vine weevil. And for the first time in a book, there are step-by-step guides to planting in flower towers, pouches, flower balls and Babyllon bowls. All in all,* Collins Easy Hanging Baskets and Window Boxes *is a truly invaluable source of reference as well as an inspiring read.*

ADRIENNE WILD

EDITOR

Garden Answers magazine

Hanging baskets

For breathtaking colour and impact, nothing can beat a well planted, well tended hanging basket. It's a sheer delight, full of life and sparkle, and it's amazing what just one basket can do for the surrounding area. Place it beside the dullest of doorways or on the starkest of patios, and a remarkable transformation takes place. Suddenly even the dingiest of spaces seems bright and welcoming. The change is instant, and almost magical.

Part of the fun of hanging baskets is their versatility. Think of them as hanging gardens and be as creative as you like. By all means plant them with a glorious medley of flowers, but you'll quickly discover how enjoyable it can be to experiment. Foliage plants have their place, either as a foil for the flowers or (especially in shady spots), as lovely plants in their own right. Or how about growing some food in the sky? There's

something very enjoyable about wandering out to the back door and reaching up to pick your own sun-ripened tomatoes or plump, red strawberries. Hung up high, the fruits are well out of the reach of most pests (including small, hungry children), so will do well.

Gardening in hanging baskets is wonderful, but if you're new to it, start slowly with just one or two baskets because you'll find that they demand a good deal of care and attention. It's one of the most labour-intensive forms of gardening, especially in the summer months when regular watering, feeding and dead-heading are essential for successful displays. But it is also one of the most rewarding, bringing cheer and interest the whole year through. And that's the real beauty of hanging baskets.

Geranium, busy lizzie (impatiens) and lobelia create a typical cottage garden mix that's perfect for this rustic setting.

CHOOSING YOUR HANGING BASKET

Basic equipment

CHOOSING YOUR HANGING BASKET

At its most basic, a hanging basket is simply a container suspended in the air, packed to overflowing with plants to provide the maximum of impact in the minimum of space. While the traditional wire baskets are the best known, new forms of planters such as flower towers and pouches have recently been introduced, greatly extending your scope for mid-air gardening. They allow you to create vertical columns of colour or, if you place a flower pouch against a wall, a kind of living plaque. The shape may be different from the conventional globe, but the effect is just as impressive.

WIRE BASKETS

The traditional wire basket is the ugly duckling of the gardening world. Nothing much to write home about when it's empty, but what a beauty when it's planted up and growing strongly. The secret lies in the open mesh design which enables you to plant the sides as well as the top of the basket to give a really full, lush effect. And the more plants you cram in, the fuller and more colourful it will look as the framework disappears under a tumbling mass of flowers and foliage. For a truly spectacular display, these are the baskets to use.

Wire baskets are made from plastic coated steel and should last for years – it's generally the chain that wears out first, but garden centres stock replacements. Some models have a flat base which help when planting up, but the rounded baskets look more natural and hold more compost. As for colours, avoid white, which sticks out like a sore thumb until the plants have grown – opt for discreet green and brown.

The next question is: "Which size hanging basket to choose?" They range from 25cm/10in to a massive 50cm/20in, but we're a bit wary of the smaller baskets. They hold fewer plants, which can limit the impact of the display, and they hold less compost, so they dry out quickly and need more frequent

A traditional wire basket (top), and its modern plastic counterpart, the 'County' basket. There are a range of linings available to suit all types of hanging baskets (above, clockwise from the top: coir, foam, moss and recycled paper).

The traditional wire basket is our firm favourite because it allows you to plant very densely from top to bottom. Once the plants bush out, the basket disappears from view under a tumbling mass of colour.

with and looks far better than moss which has been allowed to dry out. You'll generally find the best quality (and best value) moss at garden centres who buy it in bulk and pack it themselves. But if all else fails and you can't get good quality moss, we've heard of enterprising gardeners raking out lawn moss and using that as a perfectly adequate substitute.

The one disadvantage with a mossed basket is that it does dry out relatively quickly, especially in warm or breezy weather, so while no other liner is as attractive as moss, most are rather better at retaining moisture. **Wool** is especially good because it has the added advantage of insulating the plants' roots from extremes of heat and cold. It's usually sold as a circular mat which is easy enough to fit, but the tough texture can be tricky to cut – a major disadvantage if you want to make holes for side planting. There is, though, a new form of wool liner that makes life a bit easier. Looking rather like a ball of extra thick string, you simply line the basket in a spiralling layer from bottom to top, pausing only to pop in the plants as you go round.

Other 'all-in-one' liners include mats made of **coir fibre**, whose brown colouring does look relatively natural but, again, it's difficult to cut. **Foam** liners are much easier, but their lurid spotted green and white appearance is enough to turn the strongest stomach. Better than either of these are the pre-formed flexible liners made from green **polythene** – side planting is simple, and they're remarkably good at retaining water. You could make your own using ordinary black polythene, though it does look rather utilitarian initially.

Alternatively, you could opt for the more rigid **recycled paper** liners which are a bit like waterproofed, corrugated cardboard. They're cheap and cheerful, but be warned – they're inflexible and are a nightmare to cut through, which does rather restrict their use.

watering. Larger baskets have room for plenty of plants, producing the most wonderful displays, and the greater volume of compost reduces watering. But they're incredibly heavy (weighing upwards of 11kg/25lb when watered), so it's essential to support them with extra strong, very securely bolted brackets.

Our firm choice is to go for a compromise. We're great fans of the 35cm/14in model which holds a good amount of compost (amazingly, 50% more than a 30cm/12in basket), has space for plenty of plants, and isn't too heavy. So watering isn't too onerous, moving them isn't too much of a chore, and you can achieve some excellent displays.

Lining wire baskets

Of course, the open mesh design of a wire basket is great for lush planting, but it does have the rather fundamental drawback of not keeping the soil in. So you'll need a liner too. **Moss** is the traditional choice and despite the many alternatives, it's still the best because nothing else produces such a natural finish. But if you're a 'green' gardener and are concerned that sphagnum moss is harvested from peat bogs, look out for the more threadlike moss which is gathered from conifer plantations and is infinitely renewable.

Whichever moss you buy, check the bag to make sure it's fresh, moist and green. It's much easier to work

CHOOSING YOUR HANGING BASKET

The closed environment of a basket bag encourages rapid growth.

Finally, there is the ultimate in liners for low maintenance gardeners. Called a **basket bag**, it's a flexible plastic liner with an integral top. You pop it in the hanging basket, fill it with compost through the top and, once full (for best results it must be well filled), plant up through the sides and top. A special watering pot is then fitted into the central hole so that the unit is effectively sealed. Water is added through the top and the enclosed environment retains warmth and moisture, encouraging rapid growth. The major advantage, though, is that evaporation is minimised, so that even in the hottest weather it should only need watering every six to eight days. Basket bags are sold in three different diameters to fit the most popular sizes of hanging baskets.

PLASTIC BASKETS

'Hanging pot' plastic baskets have a number of practical advantages. They don't need lining, they're quick and easy to plant up (just pop a few plants in the top), and watering is less of a worry since there's no evaporation from the sides. Most of them also have a clip-on saucer which not only minimises drips but also acts as a water reservoir.

Plastic 'pot' baskets are often relatively wide and shallow. Make the most of their shape by using bushy trailers like these pink 'Surfinia' petunias to create a full, lush effect.

They're also long-lasting and good value for money. But, because most models can only be planted at the top, you'll never achieve the lush and abundant style of a wire basket, and they can look rather stark until trailing plants begin to disguise the sides. They're generally available in plain (and often rather shiny) brown, green or white, though one enterprising manufacturer has recently launched a rather stylish terracotta coloured version, tastefully decorated with classical designs.

There are other innovations too. One range of plastic baskets incorporates four side holes which can be planted up for a fuller effect, and even more spectacular displays can be created with the 'County' style of basket. The ribbed sides allow for a very dense planting, while the small water reservoir in the base helps to keep the basket well-watered and evenly moist.

SELF WATERING BASKETS

These are ingenious things. On the outside they look like ordinary plastic baskets, but at the base is a water reservoir, separated from the compost by a platform covered in capillary matting. Water seeps up through

the matting, so the compost is always moist. All you have to do is top up the reservoir once a week or so. And even though they hold less compost than conventional baskets, this doesn't restrict the number of plants you can use, because the regular supply of water more than compensates.

We don't advise that you use them in winter when evaporation is slow and in wet weather the compost can become waterlogged, but they work superbly well in summer and they're a great labour saving device for busy (or absent-minded) gardeners.

BABYLLON BOWLS

These innovative planters (and yes, they are spelt this way!) are handsome objects even when unplanted, forming a circle of wide, curved prongs. These are made of nylon coated steel, and have a pleasing sculptural quality. The bowl fits into a special wall-mounted bracket, so chains aren't needed and there's no swinging about on a windy day. They also swivel easily so that you can rotate them for even growth.

Planting is remarkably easy (see pages 34-5), especially if you are using larger pot-grown bedding plants, and the bowl is quickly transformed into a ball of colour. They do cost slightly more than traditional baskets and, at present, are only available in one width (28cm/11in), but they're well worth looking out for.

FLOWER POUCHES

These are basically small sacks of heavy duty plastic (25cm/10in wide by 50cm/20in deep), which you fill with compost, ready for planting up. Cheap and cheerful, they hang flat against the wall, looking something like a miniature growbag, taking up very little space and making a delightful splash of colour. Planting up is slightly fiddly despite the pre-cut holes, but the key to success is to firm in the compost really well and to water thoroughly – it's essential that the entire tube is evenly watered through the growing season. They're sometimes sold as kits which include water retention gel and slow-release fertiliser to make them even easier to look after. Try one – they're fun, extremely useful where space is at a premium, and you can achieve some surprisingly good results.

FLOWER TOWERS

These are hanging, flexible tubes (approximately 20cm/8in wide by 30cm/12in deep), with a built-in water reservoir. They can take up to 40 plants and create a spectacular column of colour. Like pouches, top-to-bottom watering is important for balanced growth, but it's less of a chore because of the water reservoir, which only needs to be topped up every few days in summer. But a word of warning – when filled with moist compost, plants and a full reservoir, they're very heavy, so it's important to check that your bracket is able to cope. If in doubt, you can always use them as a freestanding feature instead.

In our experience, flower towers work best as summer planters, because in winter the compost can become waterlogged rather too easily. To prevent this, it is essential that the reservoir is emptied after each watering.

Flower towers (above) and wall-mounted flower pouches (below) are welcome new players in the hanging baskets game. Plant them generously from top to bottom for a spectacular column of colour.

WHICH COMPOST?

For results like this – vibrant plants, bursting with health and vigour – a good compost is essential.

WHICH COMPOST?

For the best results in any hanging container, you must use a good compost. Don't even think about using garden soil, which will compact down in the container, is entirely the wrong consistency for good root growth, and could be harbouring pests and diseases. Plants hate it, and it makes for miserable, stunted growth.

Peat-based multipurpose compost is excellent value and has a light, open texture that encourages superb plant growth. It holds water well, but if you let a wire or plastic basket get thoroughly dry, it can be difficult to re-wet (water rushes over the dry surface rather than penetrating). The best option in this case is to plunge the basket in water until it is thoroughly saturated.

You could, of course, opt for the composts that are specially formulated for hanging baskets. These contain wetting agents which allow the compost to take up water even when partially dry. But they can be expensive and are available only in smaller sizes, so it can be an expensive option compared to buying large bags of multipurpose compost, for example.

You can also use a traditional John Innes soil-based compost (JI No.2 is fine for basket plants). It's far heavier (so check that the bracket can cope), but it retains water very well and is easy to re-wet if you've let it dry out. Quality can vary though, so to be on the safe side, make sure you buy a brand made by a member of the John Innes Manufacturers' Association. Cheapest of all, try using the compost from growbags. It's good stuff, though you'll find that it's rather more free draining than other composts and will need slightly more frequent watering.

The latest thing in composts, though, is one that incorporates an insecticide which prevents attacks from a host of plant pests including aphids and vine weevil. Not for organic gardeners, admittedly, but for the low maintenance gardener it could be a real boon.

CHOOSING BRACKETS

When buying a bracket, make sure it is big enough, and strong enough, for the job in hand. They're sold in a range of sizes for different diameter baskets, to ensure that the arm holds the planted basket clear of the wall. Be wary of the cheaper plastic brackets, which aren't very tough and can become brittle with age. Plastic coated steel versions are much safer. You can even buy more sophisticated models with built-in pulleys which make watering far easier. You simply lower the basket to a convenient height, water it, then raise it back to its display height. Others have simple security devices which enable you to padlock the basket and bracket together. And for safety's sake, whichever bracket you buy, anchor it firmly to the wall using rawlplugs and galvanised screws and check that it is secure before hanging up your basket.

For safety's sake, use a sturdy, well-secured bracket.

they will benefit from a couple of feeds come the warmer spring weather.

WATER RETENTION GRANULES

Another great idea for low maintenance gardeners. When mixed with water, the sugar-like crystals swell up into a frogspawn-like gel which you add to the compost at planting time. These little reservoirs release water to the plants as needed, and can halve the number of times you have to water. But they're not suitable for winter plantings, since there's a danger that the compost could become waterlogged and cause rots. And please be aware that you shouldn't leave the granules where small children can get at them. They look awfully like sugar, and swell up if swallowed; they don't do any permanent harm, but it would be a very uncomfortable experience.

Water retention granules (right) are tremendously useful for summer plantings, especially in the traditional wire baskets which can lose moisture at an alarming rate in hot weather. Mix them into the compost (above) before planting up.

WHICH FERTILISER?

All composts contain enough fertiliser to help the plants establish over the first few weeks of growth, but after that it's up to you. You will find that vigorous summer plants, rushing into leaf and flower, and competing for nutrients in this highly artificial environment, really do need their food.

The easiest way to feed summer plantings is to add slow-release fertiliser to the compost when planting up. Sold as loose granules, sticks or tablets, it is gradually released in minute quantities throughout the growing season. It's as simple as that, and it works brilliantly. In our experience, the granules have a slight edge because once mixed into the compost they distribute fertiliser evenly throughout the basket. Tablets and sticks tend to concentrate the feed around them.

The slightly more time consuming (and traditional) method is to use a powder or liquid fertiliser once a week. Pick a high potash fertiliser such as liquid tomato food, which has the optimum balance of nutrients for flower production. The liquid feeds are slightly easier to use, since powders can take time to dissolve properly. This is the cheapest of all ways of feeding your plants, costing just a few pence a week.

Don't forget that autumn and winter baskets, which don't grow as much, don't need any food at all, though

TIPS

✔ *Some plastic baskets are sold with clip-on plastic hangers. These rarely last more than one season, the small clips breaking easily as the plastic becomes brittle with age. Far better, if possible, to buy models fitted with metal chains, which should last for years.*

✔ *If you've a surplus of sphagnum moss after planting up, don't throw it away. It will last almost indefinitely if sealed in a clear plastic bag.*

✔ *Some garden centres now sell an artificial moss substitute which looks rather like springy strands of thin grass. It's undoubtedly a useful alternative, though you might find the colour somewhat lurid.*

✔ *Half-baskets are a great space-saving idea, taking up very little room and fitting directly onto the wall. Their only drawback is that they hold fewer plants than a conventional basket, and less compost, so they tend to dry out more quickly.*

GROWING SUCCESS

Growing success

Hanging baskets are the demanding babies of the gardening world, and summer baskets are especially time-consuming. Regular watering, regular feeding, and the constant removal of spent blooms are the order of the day if they're to flourish.

Not an easy task (and we take our hats off to those gardeners who manage to virtually obscure their houses under a sea of colourful summer baskets), but utterly rewarding. Because when all the hard work pays off and they're bright and bonny and beaming, you can rightly take a real pride in your achievement.

So measure the time you have available, and plan the size of your hanging basket family accordingly. With careful planting and routine maintenance, even the novice basket-gardener can achieve magnificent results.

CHOOSING YOUR PLANTS

If you're not growing from seed, then you'll need to buy young plants for your hanging baskets. They're available at various stages of growth from garden centres and from mail order suppliers who advertise in gardening magazines and newspapers.

Small **plug-grown** plants are particularly good value for money. They're individually grown in miniature cells of compost and it's very easy to pop them out and plant them directly into the basket. If you buy them mail order, they usually arrive in mid spring and the basket can be planted up immediately, though you'll have to keep it in a light spot indoors until there's no longer any danger of frost in your area. The great advantage is that by the time the basket has been hardened off and you put it outside, the plants will have grown so much that your basket will have instant impact. Alternatively, if you don't have room for a basket indoors, transfer the plug plants to individual 9cm/3½in pots and grow them on a sunny windowsill indoors until you're ready to plant up.

From late spring onwards you'll find larger plants on sale at garden centres. These more mature plants are sold in **strips**, **boxes** and **pots**. Strip-grown plants are the cheapest, but they're generally pretty small, and because several plants are sown together, root damage is inevitable when splitting them up and they'll take longer to get established.

Potted plants are the most mature, and particularly useful for instant results, but they are the most expensive way of planting up a basket, and the bushy head of foliage can be tricky to insert through the sides of a wire basket. So you might prefer to compromise by using cell-grown box bedding, which is just a larger version of plug plants, grown in individual cells. Again, they're easy to pop out of the cells and can be planted up without damaging the roots.

When you're buying plants by mail order, there's no way of telling what quality they will be, but in our experience they are usually pretty immaculate. If not, complain loudly. Any good company will immediately send replacements. Plant them up immediately – don't let them hang around in the packaging. At the garden centre or nursery, you should pick out the very best plants available. Look for sturdy, bushy specimens with a healthy glow about them. Reject any that are spindly, show any sign of pests or diseases or are thoroughly dry (they'll feel very light when you pick them up).

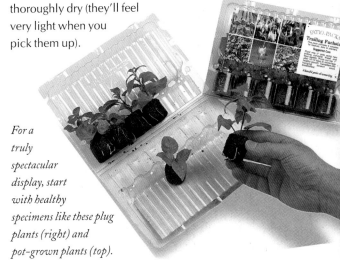

For a truly spectacular display, start with healthy specimens like these plug plants (right) and pot-grown plants (top).

PLANTING UP

Check the root system too – a few roots emerging from the bottom of the container is a good sign, a mass of roots indicates that the plant should have been re-potted long ago and is suffering.

If you're choosing bulbs for spring baskets, select the firmest and plumpest. Forget any that are soft or have started to sprout. And when buying bulbs like bluebells and snowdrops, check that they have been commercially grown rather than collected from the wild – responsible suppliers will always state this on the packet.

PLANTING UP

Although you'll be itching to get going, the first thing to do is to water your plants thoroughly and leave them for at least an hour. This helps to keep the rootball intact when you remove it from its container, and makes it easier to gently tease apart strip-grown plants with a minimum of root damage. It also helps the plants to get off to a better start in the basket – if it's not moist to start with, the rootball will be very slow to take up moisture, however well you water the basket after planting.

Now let's take a look at the different methods of planting up different containers, starting with our personal favourite, the mossed wire basket.

PLANTING UP A MOSSED WIRE BASKET

This is the method of multi-layer planting which produces the most colourful, fully rounded baskets of all. Planting up the sides is fiddly work, but these additional plants make such an impact that it's well worth the extra few minutes of effort.

The basic planting method is illustrated in our step-by-step guide to a low maintenance, mossed basket on pages 24-5, but there are a few points worth noting:
- If you're using granular slow-release fertiliser or water crystals, don't forget to mix them with the compost before planting up.
- Firm the moss down against the mesh so that it makes a good, thick layer that retains both compost and water.
- For a good, even cover round the base of the basket, set smaller plants such as lobelia or brachycome 7.5cm/3in apart. More vigorous plants such as helichrysum or petunia should be set 15cm/6in apart.
- You may only have room for two layers round the sides of smaller baskets, but the larger ones can take three layers or even four.
- If a plant has an extra-full head of foliage and it's difficult to persuade it through the mesh without damaging it, try the tube trick. Lay the plant on a piece of polythene or newspaper and roll it up as tightly as you dare without crushing it. The tube can then be passed through the wire with a minimum of damage. Once the foliage is through, gently remove the wrapping.
- Be extra-generous with the moss around the top of the basket. Make a good, thick, tightly wadded layer that will act as a wall when you're watering, so that water is contained rather than spilling over the top.

Whether planting up a wire basket (left) or a flower pouch (right) it's important to water plants well before you start.

PLANTING USING OTHER LINERS

Baskets with wool or cocoa fibre mat liners are planted in much the same way as mossed baskets, and the only problem you're likely to encounter is when making additional planting holes. Wool is reasonably pliable and can be cut *in situ*, but if you're using a cocoa fibre mat it's easier to make the holes beforehand – just cut a cross through the fabric, open out the flaps, then push them back into position after planting.

Alternatively, you can just plant through the pre-cut slits that help the liner fit snugly in the basket, though you won't get quite as full an effect. And don't forget to ease the liner back around each plant to prevent compost from washing out.

PLANTING UP OTHER HANGING CONTAINERS

Planting up plastic pot baskets is the easiest job in the world because all you have to worry about is the plants that go in the top. But make sure that you include a number of trailing plants to cascade over and disguise the sides. You'll find a step-by-step guide to planting a plastic basket on pages 30-31). Open-sided plastic baskets like the 'County' type are pretty simple too – the ribs are flexible, making it easy to insert even quite large plants without damaging them.

Flower towers and flower pouches are also pretty quick to plant up, and you'll find the methods illustrated in our step-by-step guides on pages 26-9. The great thing to remember here is to really cram the compost down so that you don't leave any air pockets.

Hanging baskets add a whole new dimension to the garden. An elegant doorway (above left) becomes hugely welcoming with its glowing basket, while the pergola baskets (left, and above right) lift the eye and complement the delights of the ground–level plantings.

AFTERCARE

From now on, the plants in the basket are entirely at your mercy, relying on you completely for their well-being – and because they're so tightly crammed together, they're especially vulnerable, spending all their lives fighting for their fair share of food and water. So it's up to you to keep up the catering standards.

WATERING

A regular and even supply of water is essential for basket plants, especially with notoriously fussy characters like fuchsias. The compost can dry out remarkably quickly in hot weather, so check them often, and don't assume they're wet if it's been raining; the dense canopy of leaves deflects most of the rain, preventing it from wetting the compost.

Most gardeners use a watering can for the job, but they can be heavy when full and it's difficult to lift them high enough to reach the basket. To overcome the problem, you can buy special pulley systems which enable you to lower the basket to waist level when you need to. Or you could use a 1 litre/2 pint plastic bottle instead of a watering can. It's far less heavy, and holds just about the right quantity of water for most baskets.

If you prefer to use the hosepipe, then keep the water pressure low. If it's too high, you can end up washing the compost out (it's happened to us and it makes a real mess). Far safer to fit a long, angled watering lance (sold by most garden centres) onto the hose – it enables you to reach the basket easily, and gives a perfect, gentle spray that won't damage the flowers. Some models can be attached to hose end feeders, so you can water and feed your baskets at the same time. The ultimate answer is to install an automatic watering system (see page 110).

For summer baskets, the best time to water is in the evening or early morning because less water will be lost through evaporation. If you possibly can, avoid watering in the heat of the day, when loss through evaporation is greatest and there's the possibility of wet plants being scorched by the blazing sun. If the worst happens and the basket dries out completely, you'll probably find it very difficult to re-wet by conventional watering. So take it down and plunge it in water for an hour or so to make sure the compost is thoroughly saturated.

Finally – good news! Winter watering is far less onerous. Rain will do the job, but in the absence of rain, weekly watering is usually sufficient.

Attaching baskets to a pulley system allows them to be lowered to a level that's convenient for easy watering.

FEEDING

This is an essential job for the spring and summer months. And it's the secret behind many a winning display. Regular feeding encourages faster growth, healthier and brighter foliage, and masses of flowers.

A hose-end lance takes the strain out of watering your hanging baskets, and delivers a fine, gentle spray.

This sumptuous globe of petunias and busy lizzies is in tip-top condition, thanks to regular watering and feeding. A hanging basket is a highly artificial environment, the densely-packed plants competing for their fair share of food and water, but regular rations will keep them growing strongly and evenly.

The simplest way to feed your hanging baskets is to add slow-release fertiliser to the compost at planting time. With most products, the rate of release is controlled by temperature, so that the warmer it is (and the faster the plants are growing), the more fertiliser is released into the compost. But they can sometimes run out of steam by late summer, so it is worth giving them a couple of liquid feeds at this time.

The alternative to slow-release fertilisers is to use a liquid feed which should be applied once a week in spring and summer. High potash fertiliser (such as liquid tomato food) is best for flowering and fruiting plants, a high nitrogen fertiliser for anything leafy like salad crops.

DEAD-HEADING

Most flowering plants produce seed, but for the basket gardener, it's a real pain. In doing so, they divert energy from flower production, and once a sufficient quantity of seed is ripe, they decide that they've fulfilled their purpose in life and gradually start to fade away. So as soon as you notice any fading blooms, dead-head them by nipping them off at the base of the stalk, to ensure plenty of flowers to come, and a neat-looking basket.

TIPS

✔ *You may not have a choice about where you position your basket, but the ideal spot for a flowery summer display is in a sheltered position, where plants won't be knocked about by wind, and away from the midday sun. Blazing sun causes rapid moisture loss, whereas morning or late afternoon sun is much kinder.*

✔ *You'll often find small plug plants at the garden centre very early in the year, but we suggest that you resist buying them until at least mid spring. If you buy too early, they can struggle because of the low light levels.*

✔ *Don't worry about the small mesh pots or fine netting surrounding the rootball of some bedding plants. Neither need be removed when planting up, since the roots will grow quite happily through the gaps.*

Dead-heading is a dull old job, but essential – just one or two faded blooms can ruin the overall appearance of a basket.

Step-by-step planting success

Hanging containers, as we've already shown, come in quite a range of designs, and each one has its own particular planting method. So if any of them are unfamiliar to you, just take a look at the following step–by–step planting sequences which, we hope, will make it all clear.

At the same time, we decided to try our hand at a little colour co-ordination, using schemes that varied from the freshness of blue and gold, to the more romantic tones of delicate pink and silver – and we think that the single-plant ball basket demonstrates just how effective such a simple planting can be.

Watching the baskets grow to full maturity was exciting and we were very pleased with the results. If you like them too, just make a note of the 'ingredients' for each recipe, pick up the plants and hardware at the garden centre, and get planting!

A low maintenance, mossed, wire hanging basket

Traditional mossed baskets have a natural charm and with careful tending will produce wonderful displays. But they lose water through evaporation very quickly and watering is a major chore, with baskets needing twice-daily watering in the height of summer.

So we decided to try a low maintenance method pioneered by Tony Andrews and his colleagues at the St Helier Parks Department in Jersey. Part of the secret lies in the ingenious watering column in the centre of the basket, made up of Hortag expanded clay granules. This helps distribute water through the basket so that all the compost is evenly watered rather than just the top (which is what often happens, especially if the compost is slightly dry).

Other secrets include the use of loam-based John Innes Compost, which retains water better than peat-based composts, and the careful selection of drought-tolerant plants. We also included water retention granules and slow-release fertiliser to eliminate the need for a weekly feed.

The basket took 25 minutes to plant up. It was extremely heavy, due to the additional weight of the John Innes compost, and needed an extra strong bracket. But it was undoubtedly easier to look after. It needed watering just once a day in the hottest of weather, and most of the time we only had to water every other day. So for beautiful results with far less hassle, have a go at this one.

HARDWARE

40cm/16in wire basket
1 large bag moss
1 piece polythene, 20cm/8in in diameter
1 kitchen roll tube
1 small bag Hortag expanded clay granules
60g/2½ oz slow-release fertiliser
4 teaspoons water retention crystals
20 litres John Innes No 2 potting compost

PLANTS
(for a warm blue, pink, purple and silver scheme)

2 x brachycome, any blue variety
2 x helichrysum petiolare
4 x petunia 'Chiffon Morn'
4 x busy lizzie (impatiens) 'Accent Pink'
3 x geranium (pelargonium) 'Century Appleblossom'
2 x verbena 'Tapien Violet'

1 Place the basket on a pot to make it stable, partially remove the chain so that it's not in the way, and line the bottom third of the basket with a well-packed, 2.5cm/1in layer of moss. Place the polythene on top of the moss.

2 Holding the tube of kitchen roll in the centre of the polythene, fill it with Hortag to approximately the top of the basket. Mix the fertiliser and water retention granules with the compost, then fill to the level of the moss.

3 Plant the brachycome and helichrysum, working from the inside and easing the foliage through the wire. Moss another third of the basket, add more compost, then plant 2 petunias and 2 busy lizzies midway above the existing plants.

4 Moss to the rim of the basket, plant the geraniums in the centre, fill in with the remaining petunias and busy lizzies, then plant the verbena and felicia around the edge. Top up with compost, firm it down, and remove the tube.

5 Water well, adding more compost if needed. Patch any gaps in the moss to prevent compost from washing out, secure the chain and hang on a very strong bracket. Take care when lifting since the basket will be very heavy.

A LOW MAINTENANCE, MOSSED, WIRE HANGING BASKET

A FLOWER TOWER

A flower tower

For the past few years, flower show visitors have flocked to the Flower Tower stand. It's a spectacle of colour, with everything from bedding plants to houseplants, herbs, strawberries and even potatoes flourishing in their towers.

But it's not just the plants – part of the attraction lies in the opportunity to see the inventor, David Hawkins in action. Given the slightest encouragement, he'll give an enthusiastic planting demonstration. David invented the tower because, as a less then keen gardener, he found he always failed with hanging baskets and decided to try to make something that would be easier to look after. The major benefit of the tower is that it reduces the frequency of watering, thanks partly to the built-in water reservoir, and also because the polythene tube minimises any loss through evaporation. In very hot weather we only had to water every other day. But the water-filled reservoir does make the tower very heavy, so make sure your bracket is strong enough to hold it.

This tower took 15 minutes to plant up. As it was early June, we used larger plants for instant effect, but if we'd started earlier in the season we would have chosen cheaper plug plants. Plugs are also rather easier to plant up, since you just fill the whole tower with compost and pop them into the planting holes. The larger rootballs of our more mature plants

dictated that planting (as the pictures show), had to be done in stages.

We were tremendously pleased with the finished result, the scaevola, in particular, looked beautiful against the contrasting flower shapes of the petunias and brachycome.

HARDWARE
flower tower
20 litres multipurpose compost
2 teaspoons water retention granules
60g/2½oz slow-release fertiliser

PLANTS
(for a rich blue scheme with just a touch of yellow)
9 x petunia 'Express Sky Blue'
2 x scaevola 'New Wonder'
2 x brachycome, any blue variety
2 x lysimachia 'Aurea'
2 x lysimachia 'Outback Sunset'
2 x helichrysum 'Variegatum'

An attractive mix of flowering and foliage plants is used in this display.

2 Continue with layers of compost and plants right to the top. A tower can accommodate up to 40 plug plants, but we used less, as our plants were already pretty big. Plant the scaevola at the top.

1 Fill the bottom quarter of the tower with compost and firm it down. Using a sharp knife, cut a cross for the first plant and ease it in so that the rootball rests on the compost. Complete the bottom layer with alternating blue and gold flowering plants.

3 Slowly add two pints of water to the compost, so that it gently soaks the soil and settles the plants in. Hang the tower in position and top up the reservoir at the base, so that water will be taken up as plants need it.

A FLOWER POUCH

A flower pouch

Although they've only been available for the past couple of years, flower pouches have become tremendously popular. They're very straightforward – basically a bag or tube of compost rather like a mini growbag, which is planted on one side and hung against a wall on a nail or bracket.

And although they are such a simple idea, they can produce the most wonderful displays. However, to ensure the best possible results, it is important to moisten the compost thoroughly before planting to make sure there are no dry pockets. To help the plants get a really firm grip on the compost, leave the bag lying down for the first three weeks after planting, setting it upright only for watering.

It's important, too, to keep the pouch evenly moist by watering generously so that water gets right to the bottom of the compost. Check by squeezing the bottom corners – water should gently trickle out.

Planting took only 15 minutes, and aftercare is pretty easy, thanks to the water retention granules and slow-release fertiliser. We planted up in early summer, using the smallest plants available at that time of year, but if you were planting up in mid to late spring, you could use cheaper plug plants.

Pouches can, of course, be used for bulky plants but we prefer the effect of more compact plants like the Petunia 'Million Bells', which is much neater than, say, Petunia 'Surfinia'. But feel free to experiment – pouches are so cheap that you can afford to.

HARDWARE
60g/2½oz slow-release fertiliser
2 teaspoons water retention granules
20 litres multipurpose compost
flower pouch

PLANTS
(for a hot colour scheme)
2 x petunia 'Million Bells', blue
3 x French marigold 'Aurora Orange'
7 x petunia 'Fantasy Red'

Small plants like these are ideal for planting in flower pouches.

1 Mix the slow-release fertiliser and water retention granules into the compost. Water until thoroughly moist. Prop the pouch upright and fill it to the top. Hold it by the handle and tap the base a few times to firm the compost down.

3 After planting up all ten slits, lift the pouch up, tap it to settle the compost down, then plant the top with the remaining two plants. Check again for any air pockets, adding more compost as necessary so that the pouch is completely full.

2 Lay the pouch flat and make a small planting hole in the compost by pushing your finger through a pre-cut slit. Ease the rootball in and firm the compost around the plant, adding a little more if necessary. Carry on to the next planting slit.

4 Whilst upright, give the pouch some more water, squeezing the bottom corners to check that it has been thoroughly watered. Place the bag flat again and grow on for three weeks. And now it's ready to be hung up on display.

A plastic hanging basket

Not only is this the easiest basket of all to plant, it is also the easiest to look after – the perfect choice for a beginner. We used the most basic type of plastic basket here, but others have built-in self-watering devices which are a great boon for busy gardeners; they generally require watering only every three days or so even in the hottest weather.

The secret of success with any plastic basket is to plant plenty of trailers around the edge. These quickly cascade over and disguise the stark appearance of the plastic. As you can see from the picture of the finished planting, the nepeta and lysimachia do a good job of disguising the basket, and their long delicate trails make a lovely finishing touch.

The basket took just 10 minutes to plant, using a cool, gentle colour scheme. Petunias in the yellow colour range have been relatively scarce until recently, but an award-winning variety called 'Prism Sunshine' has just been introduced. This is widely available and would make a similar striking topping for the basket as the one we used. The frothy infill of white busy lizzie and yellow-centred lysimachia adds to what, all in all, we feel is quite a romantic picture. You could create a similar effect using lemon-yellow tuberous begonias in the upright rather than cascading form, together with smaller-flowered white semperflorens begonias and a haze of white lobelia.

HARDWARE
45g/2oz slow-release fertiliser
15 litres multipurpose compost
25cm/10in plastic hanging planter

PLANTS
(for a romantic, pale yellow scheme)
2 x nepeta/glechoma 'Variegata'
2 x nierembergia 'Mont Blanc'
2 x petunia 'Frenzy Butter Cream'
2 x lysimachia 'Aurea'
4 x busy lizzie (impatiens) 'Accent White' (you could use two larger plants instead)

1 To make life easier, add slow-release fertiliser. This can be added to the compost in advance, but in plastic pots it's just as easy (and probably less messy) to put the compost in the basket and then mix in the fertiliser.

3 Fill in any gaps around the plants with compost, firming it gently round the rootballs. Plant the centre, alternating the petunias and busy lizzies. Firm them down and add more compost, if necessary, to any dips and hollows.

2 Since the trailing plants are the most important, it's better to start with these then work inwards. We alternated between the nepeta, lysimachia and nierembergia. You can remove the hanger if it's in the way, though it's not essential.

4 Water thoroughly. If you're using a self-watering model, continue adding water until it starts to seep out of the overflow holes. Other models have integral saucers which should be clipped on before hanging the basket up.

A FLOWER BALL

A flower ball

If you want to grow something to really impress the neighbours, this is the one to go for. A ball of colour that looks spectacular for months on end, and something that looks incredibly difficult to achieve, though thankfully it's not.

Here we've used a specially made ball basket with an integral pot that acts as a sump for easier watering. You could make your own very similar version from two wire baskets. Fix a 9cm/3½in plant pot into the top half (to make a reservoir) before adding the compost, then when the two halves are planted, wire them together to make your sphere.

As for plants, we've chosen busy lizzies because they have a very neat habit and grow into a particularly well-formed, close-knit ball. Semperflorens begonias would also look good, but bushier plants such as petunias are too vigorous and you wouldn't get the neatly rounded effect. The other advantage with busy lizzies, of course, is that they are wonderful in sun or shade, so our vivid red ball could lighten up even the gloomiest of spots.

Planting is pretty laborious, although it shouldn't provide much difficulty for anyone who has mastered the art of side-planting a traditional wire basket. In total, our basket took 45 minutes to complete – a long time perhaps, but well worth it for the pleasure it gave us when it came into full flower a few weeks later.

HARDWARE
3 teaspoons water retention granules
35 litres multipurpose compost
basket ball

PLANTS
(for a dazzling red display)
16 x busy lizzie (impatiens) 'Accent Scarlet'
   (plugs or strips of small plants)

Small plants like these busy lizzies are ideal for planting in a flower ball.

1 First mix the water granules with the compost. If using the fibre liners that come with some kits, make a series of eight evenly spaced holes in each. Rest one basket on a pot to steady it, and fill with compost to the first layer of holes.

2 Ease the first plant through the hole so that the rootball rests on the compost. Complete the planting of the first layer with three more busy lizzies, then top up with more compost to the second layer, firm down and plant the second level.

3 Once the planting is completed, fill to the very top with more of the compost mix. Firm it down, then add a little more to make a small dome in the centre. This compost will fill any gaps when you join the baskets together.

4 Plant the other basket and give them both a thorough watering. Attach the baskets to each other with one small loop tie. Don't make it too tight, to allow for the hinge action when the two baskets are closed together.

5 Holding a basket in each hand, gently close them together. Despite what you may fear, this won't be a disaster because the moist compost holds firm. Tie the baskets together, attach the chain and hang on an extra strong bracket.

A Babyllon bowl

The Babyllon bowl is a totally different type of basket. It was invented by Richard Conway, an engineer and keen gardener who decided to experiment with new forms of planters. His early prototypes of the bowl were so successful that all the neighbours wanted one, so Richard set up in business to make them. His ingenious invention now sells in many countries around the world.

The major advantage of the bowl is that it is supported from the base so that it doesn't swing around in the wind. It also looks rather more attractive than a conventional basket because there are no obtrusive chains in the way. It's easy to plant, too, by simply sliding the plants between the prongs and packing them in with moss.

We decided to use large cell-grown bedding which is slightly cheaper than 9cm/3 1/2in size pot-grown plants. Plug plants are rather too small for this planting technique because they need a lot of moss to hold them in position. For an even less expensive option, use strip-grown plants, inserting the whole strip rather than breaking it up. Water them well first, then gently bend the strips to fit the curve of the bowl. Two or three strips will be sufficient for the first layer. Once completed, build the second layer on top overlapping the joints like brickwork. Finally, add compost to the rest and plant the top with two more strips. Apart from being quick and easy, the other advantage of using strip bedding is that you don't need to use any moss!

The bowl was planted up rather late, during July, but it still managed to look spectacular until the first frosts.

HARDWARE
1 Babyllon bowl
15 litres multipurpose compost

PLANTS
1 large bag moss
12 x busy lizzie (impatiens), any pink variety
3 x fuchsia, any pink variety

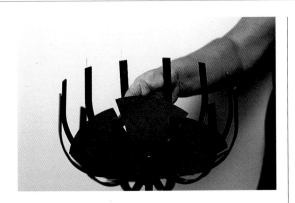

1 Place the bowl on a secure base, such as a large flower pot. Here the bowl is supported on a special display stand (which is sold with the free-standing rather than the wall-mounted models). Position the fibre liner (provided with the bowl) in the bottom.

3 Although smaller plug sized plants can be used, pot or cell grown plants are preferable because larger root balls are better secured by the prongs. Slide a fuchsia between alternate prongs, resting the rootball on the compost. Fill the remaining 3 gaps with busy lizzie plants.

2 As with any planter, it is advisable to thoroughly water the busy lizzies and fuchsias before planting. Research has shown that dry plants suffer a considerable check in growth – up to 6 weeks in some instances. Then cover the liner with a 2.5cm/1in layer of compost.

4 Pack moss between the rootballs. Plant the second layer using 6 more busy lizzie plants, positioning the plants above the gaps of the first layer. Pack in more moss and fill the centre with compost. Plant the top with the remaining busy lizzies and water well.

ACKNOWLEDGMENTS
Many thanks to Richard Conway of Textice Ltd for supplying these step-by-step photographs. All the other step-by-step planting guides were compiled with the help of Brian Smith of Woodlea Nurseries. We are most grateful to Brian who planted and maintained all the planters at his nurseries.

PLANTING IDEAS

Planting ideas

Hanging baskets are one of life's frivolities. They're not actually essential. But neither is champagne, or perfume, or a box of chocolates. A spot of indulgence never hurt anyone. And it's a luxury that you can enjoy all year round. Summer displays, with spectacular baskets brimming with flowers, are undoubtedly the showiest of all, but there's no reason why you can't have baskets that are almost as lovely through winter and into spring. In sunny spots and shady spots, using flower, foliage, fruit and herbs, there's a basket for every season.

Summer is the time when you can achieve the most spectacular displays, like this globe of petunia, lobelia and busy lizzie (above), but winter and spring baskets can be almost equally attractive. For a cool, refreshing effect, try an all–white scheme. Here, white petunias sparkle beautifully.

SUMMER COLOUR

Summer is the time when you can really go to town with your baskets, using a mass of fabulous bedding plants to produce some truly spectacular effects. It's a terrific way of being creative, of expressing yourself, and one of the best things about it is the opportunity to play around with colour; while a random mix can be very attractive, a more careful choice can make a magnificent picture.

Keeping it cool

Starting as cool as possible, have you ever thought of planting an all-white scheme? It can be a really sparkling affair using, for example, the crisp whites of petunias and busy lizzies. White lobelia, too, would look good with the petunias, but you may have to weed out the odd stray blue flower, which always seem to creep in. For an even more ghostly effect, add in some of the silvers that have a white glitter to them, like the cut-leaved *Cineraria/Senecio* 'Silver Dust' or metallic silver *Lamium* 'Hermann's Pride'.

Lemon or gold with white is another lovely cool combination, looking particularly refreshing on a baking summer's day. A number of nasturtiums will give you a clear lemon-gold, notably 'Whirlybird Cream'

SUMMER COLOUR

A good deal of heat is generated by the fiery scarlet petunias in this basket, tempered by a cool scattering of white lobelia.

All shades of pink, from the very palest, through rose pink to lilac-tinted, mix beautifully here, to create a soft, dreamy scheme, using a mix of petunia, lobelia and busy lizzie.

and 'Primrose Jewel', both of them the compact forms which are so suitable for baskets. Pale gold petunias and lemony shades of French marigold would fit in well too, together with a gold-leaved trailer like *Lamium* 'Gold Nuggets' or *Lysimachia* 'Aurea'.

For a great mixer with lemon and white, how about a touch of blue? This is a colour theme much used for breakfast ware – there's a rise-and-shine, cheerful feel to it. There are lots of excellent blues to choose from too, including the yellow-centred daisies of felicia, and blue and white *Lobelia* 'Riviera Blue Splash'. For stronger, less hazy colour, pick out one of the true blue petunias like 'Sky Blue'. In fact, all shades from blue to deepest violet are tremendously versatile, with the chameleon ability to fit into any scheme, from the coolest to the very hottest. They're gregarious colours, taking on the character of the company they mix with.

Getting warmer

Pinks, apricots and peaches make a wonderful basis for warm, dreamy schemes, and they're out there in abundance with petunias, begonias, busy lizzies and diascias. But stick to the softer pastel tones to keep the picture gentle (if it helps, have a packet of sugared almonds in mind).

A scattering of white is almost *de rigueur* in these romantic schemes (rather like the gypsophila in a bridal bouquet), and busy lizzies, lobelia and nierembergia will all supply it as a pretty backdrop to larger flowers. You could use some of the softer-coloured trailers, rather than plain green; white-variegated ivy and plectranthus for instance, or, best of all, the silky pearl grey of helichrysum. Blues and lilacs will fit in well here too, so long as you restrict them to the pastel shades.

If you want something even warmer, how about a basket centred on shades of gold? It's not, oddly, a very widely used theme, so you could be breaking new ground in your neighbourhood. There are some beautiful, butter gold petunias like 'Summer Sun' that are well worth tracking down (usually via the seedsmen), and feathery bidens with its scatter of gold stars is always a winner. Try sumptuous tuberous begonias, dripping with huge double blooms, that come in all shades from the palest, to the most electric gold. Then there are marigolds, starry asteriscus, golden forms of shade-loving mimulus, and the buttercup flowers of lysimachia. Shades of gold are much easier to put together than, say, shades of blue or pink, and you can create a basket with a real glow to it.

Catching fire

Now that the first flames have ignited with our golden basket, let's fan them up to a real blaze, using some of the boldest colours in the bedding plant palette.

One of the easiest of all bonfires can be created using flowers in the red/orange/yellow range, with a few

S U M M E R   C O L O U R

Purple petunias are deliciously scented, and look especially rich when mixed with crimson geraniums and purple verbenas to create a hot, dramatic scheme.

For a real bonfire glow, exploit the superb colour range of gazanias; from gold, through all the oranges, to tawny reds and browns (below).

crimson geraniums, and mix in a few purple verbenas whose pincushion flowers contrast so well with the petunias' simple trumpets. You could also add just a dash of orange and crimson from 'Empress of India', a jewel-like, dark-leaved nasturtium. Leave to smoulder against a light-coloured wall.

Magenta is another incredibly dominant colour, and while you could choose to give it quieter companions, it's great fun to be rather bolder with it. Try it with scarlet and with one of the brighter pinks. In the garden this would be far too prominent a colour theme, distracting from other less flamboyant plantings, but in the solitary confinement of a hanging basket it works remarkably well.

That's the great thing about baskets – they're a kind of playground for colour experiments, and it's a game that you are always going to enjoy.

touches of scarlet. Nasturtiums are invaluable here, with a huge range of shades including some lovely burnt oranges. For the reds, choose the clear shades that have no hint of pink to them – in the geranium family, for example, there are several reds that almost cross the borderline to orange.

Deeper colours bring more drama to the picture, and foremost among these are purple petunias, with their velvet texture and as a bonus, a heady scent that's missing from most other colours. There's a slightly wicked, voluptuous quality to them, and they mix beautifully with a whole host of other strong colours. Try them with deep

Making the most of flower towers and pouches

Flower towers and pouches have brought a whole new dimension to the hanging gardens game. Pouches make a very impressive plaque when hung against a wall or fence, while towers hang freestyle, forming a long waterfall of colour that no other type of hanging basket can quite match.

If you haven't yet seen them in action – at a flower show for instance, or in someone else's garden – then take a look at the plantings pictured here. From the simplest to the most complex plant combinations, they really can be tremendously effective, making a huge combination to the summer scene.

A wonderful way to exploit popular red, white and blue. The combination is one that gardeners have loved since the dawn of the hanging basket era.

And it couldn't be simpler to put together. The geraniums are the continental or 'balcon' type that flower so incredibly abundantly from early summer right through to the first frosts, with a lovely loose, airy habit. Dainty lobelia flowers form a frothy infill, with a predominance of white to keep the picture light and deliciously lively.

To keep this pouch scheme looking good, deadhead the geraniums regularly, to keep them in full production, and use bush lobelias rather than trailing varieties – trailing lobelias put on so much growth that they would start to compete with the geraniums and spoil the effect.

A warm, sumptuous scheme, with the colours arranged in broad bands rather than an even mix. The pouch is topped with bright pink busy lizzies and continental geraniums, shading down to a midriff of blue bush lobelias, followed by a final layer of paler pink petunias.

Notice, too, how the introduction of a couple of contrasting colours can be used to enhance a scheme that relies on a fairly limited colour range, with apricot busy lizzies and one scarlet petunia peeping out from the top band. The purple-toned white petunias, too, add just a touch of lightness.

A beautiful, classy pouch, using cool clear colours highlighted by warmer blues and violets, the colour changes flowing together to give an almost spiralling effect.

Osteospermums provide a good scattering of starry daisies, their buttery gold shading through to the more acidic tones of Lamium 'Gold Nuggets' and pale gold-variegated ivy. Blue lobelia and soft lavender ageratum take the middle ground, making a good contrast with the crisper colours around them. The whole scheme is topped off by a jaunty hat of one of the prettiest marigolds of all time – the creamy 'French Vanilla'. And if you're a fan of these more subtly-coloured marigolds (we are), then clear yellow 'Yellow Boy', at a demure 2.5cm/5in, would look lovely added to the planting.

Geraniums are superb container plants, easily coping if you're away for a few days, and the trailing ivy-leaved varieties are perfect for a flower tower.

Here a mix of colour creates a warm, rosy glow, with just a touch of white from the lovely cerise-edged 'Mexicana' (also sold as 'Rouletta'). These are relatively compact forms creating a shapely column of colour, but if you wanted something more explosive, you could use continental or 'balcon' geraniums with their starbursts of single flowers on extra-long stems.

Geraniums are hard-working plants, and if deadheaded regularly, this tower will be in full flower production right through to the end of summer and into early autumn.

For a real waterfall of colour in a flower tower, you can't beat fuchsias, the flowers trembling and dancing in the slightest breath of wind. But be sure to select a trailing variety like 'La Campanella' featured here, rather than the more upright forms. There are plenty to choose from, two or our favourites being white and carmine 'Cascade', which does precisely that, and vigorously trailing 'Marinka' with its simple, rich red flowers.

For best results, keep well watered and deadhead regularly. And don't forget that fuchsias will thrive just as well in a shady spot as in full sun.

WINTER WARMERS

When the summer show is fading, and frosts threaten, don't just dismantle your baskets and store them away. Use them to house schemes that will be a delight from autumn right through to late spring, and doubly delightful because they need an absolute minimum of care. A little dead-heading, the occasional watering if the weather is exceptionally dry, and that's it. There is no need for feeding, and there will be very few pests to worry about until spring. Nothing could be easier, and while winter baskets will never be as colourful as summer displays, you can create some exceedingly pretty pictures.

For bold, bright, winter flowers, your greatest allies are the **winter pansies**, giving a good show of bloom through any mild spells, and flowering their hearts out in spring. At the very simplest, you could plant up a basket with just one or two complementary colours – lemon and white, say, for a cool look, or burnt orange and bright red for a really fiery combination. But the colour range is so vast that they team up beautifully with other winter plants. Say you want a gold theme for instance. Easy. Top the basket with a young plant of *Euonymus* 'Emerald 'n' Gold', fill in with gold pansies (there are quite a few shades to choose from but the variety with the central black 'eye' has the most impact and will provide the best contrast with other plants). Add gold/white *Lamium* 'Gold Nuggets' or variegated golden thyme, and finish the whole thing off with a generous skirt of gold-variegated ivy. Lovely – and it will look good all through winter.

Winter pansies (left), with their incredible colour range, are invaluable for winter baskets. Heathers too (top) bring warmth and cheer to the chilliest of days.

This scheme would work just as well with the pansies' daintier cousin, the **viola**. The colours are slightly more limited in the winter varieties, and it's a flower that peeks at you rather than staring boldly like the pansies, but it's a lovely plant for a basket that's close to eye level. It pays to plant up pansies and violas while there's still a little warmth in the world, from mid-September or so. This encourages them to get into their flowering stride before the onset of winter, so that they'll put out more flowers through any mild spells. And don't panic if they collapse and look thoroughly woebegone in frosty weather – they soon recover.

Not quite so showy, but utterly reliable for winter flower, are **heathers**. Our favourites are forms of *Erica carnea*, which sail through the harshest weather and will happily grow in any multipurpose compost. They're low-growing, too, which makes them eminently suitable for a basket, and the flower spikes have great delicacy and refinement. One of the most effective heather plantings we've ever seen was with a most unlikely partner – **ornamental cabbage**. It's hard to imagine two more contrasting plants, but they worked beautifully together, the ruffled solidity of the cabbages, in warm shades of purple, pink and white, emphasised by a delicate infill of pink and white flowering heathers.

Foliage

The other great source of winter colour for baskets is the ever-increasing range of foliage plants on offer in autumn from nurseries and garden centres. 'Foliage' sounds a bit dull, but when you look at the incredible colour range, you'll be amazed.

King of trailers, and absolutely indispensable for winter displays, is the **ivy** in all its glorious forms, from plain green to white- or gold-variegated. For gentler, more compact trails (edge-breakers really), take a look at **lysimachia** – 'Goldilocks' is a particularly splendid yellow-gold. Or at the versatile **lamiums** – again, a lovely acid gold from 'Gold Nuggets', a frosty white patina from 'White Nancy', and a mosaic of silver and green from 'Hermann's Pride'.

Ajugas, too, will spill from the rim of a basket, and here the colour gets especially riotous, rising to a crescendo from the purple tints of white-variegated 'Burgundy Glow', through the dramatic black/purple of 'Atropururea', to the extraordinary green, cream and pink extravaganza of 'Rainbow'.

For the top of the basket, there's an enormous choice. **Dwarf conifers** make a neat and formal topping, or you might prefer the more rounded silhouettes of evergreens such as **euonymus** (some terrifically bright gold variegations here), and tiny-leaved *Cotoneaster microphyllus* and *Lonicera* **'Baggesen's Gold'**.

Hebes are another neat way of rounding off a basket, particularly the domed silver-grey *Hebe pagei*. Or possibly a well-grown **sage** plant, in a range of colours from white- or gold-variegated to the various forms that are gently suffused with purple. Young plants of **skimmia** are useful, too, especially if you choose one with a substantial crop of long-lasting red berries.

Ivy, euonymus and red-berried gaultheria (top) are ideal for winter baskets, while the dense rosettes of ornamental cabbage (above) make a grand display in a low level basket.

WINTER WARMERS

THE TENDER TOUCH

If you live in a mild area, or in a city, where temperatures are higher than in the average garden, you can extend the range of plants for your winter baskets by using those that are on the borderlines of hardiness, which can survive very cold weather, but not a severe frost.

One of the prettiest is the indoor *Cyclamen persicum*, available from early autumn and sold as a cool room plant. The smaller varieties are available in a number of colours in the white/pink/magenta range. They make a lovely topping for a sheltered basket, and some are very sweetly scented, so sniff before you buy. The new 'Miracle' miniatures flower until Christmas, and have an amazing scent.

Equally pretty is the winter cherry, *Solanum capsicastrum*, with its bright, beady berries maturing from yellow to scarlet which is usually sold as a Christmas pot plant. But keep children away from the berries, which are poisonous.

Silver-leaved cineraria (now, technically, *Senecio*), is another pretty plant that will survive in warmer areas – a terrific filler plant. The cut-leaved 'Silver Dust' is especially good and is a beautiful pale silver that is almost white.

And two more for good measure, for larger baskets. Try the rose-purple heather *Erica gracilis*, and the ubiquitous *Hebe 5 franciscana* 'Variegata' – you'll never find it labelled thus, but it's instantly recognisable by its cream-edged leaves and mauve-blue flowers. If you're dubious about trying any of these plants, just check the winter displays outside local offices and pubs – if they thrive for them, they'll do equally well for you.

You will need a few filler plants to ensure interest while the basket is becoming established. One of the most handsome is maple-leaved **Heuchera** 'Palace Purple', a mournful deep purple that looks wonderful if you team it up with golden foliage. One of the most beguiling is **gaultheria**, forming hummocks of small leaves which turn bronze in cold weather, with a scattering of large red berries. And evergreen herbs are invaluable – **thyme** forms aromatic mats of tiny leaves in a wide range of colours, young **rosemary** plants add blue-grey spires, and the **curry plant**, *Helichrysum italicum* contributes its silvery needles.

WINTER BASKET CHECK LIST

Plant generously. Little growth will be made until spring, so plant much more densely than you would in a summer basket. Use the biggest plants available to give instant impact.

Water only when absolutely necessary. Overwatering can cause waterlogging and rotting, but you should never let the basket dry out completely. So check the compost during any prolonged dry spells, or after windy weather which can draw moisture from the plants via the leaves.

Dead-head regularly. Winter flowering pansies and violas, in particular, should have faded blooms removed to encourage further flowering.

Don't feed baskets until spring. Plants put on very little growth over winter, needing only the fertiliser that is already present in the compost.

Protect baskets in severe weather. If severe weather is forecast, it's a wise precaution to cover baskets with horticultural fleece to prevent them from freezing up. If, however, it's already too late and the basket has been frozen solid for more than a couple of days, move it to a more sheltered position for a while. A cold greenhouse or garage is ideal, but a cool porch or bedroom will do equally well. It's important that the basket thaws gradually. Frozen plant cells can collapse if they're defrosted too quickly, so never put the basket in a warm place.

Site baskets in as sheltered a position as possible. This limits the damage that strong winds can do, cuts down the likelihood of the basket freezing up, and encourages just that little extra growth through winter.

Low-growing ajuga is available in a huge range of leaf colours, including beetroot-tinged 'Jungle Beauty'.

SPRING SPECIALS

If you didn't get around to planting up baskets in autumn, there's still time to create stunning spring displays by snapping up some of the lovely plants on offer in garden centres from early spring onwards. They'll be in tip-top condition, saving you the bother of nursing them through winter.

Winter pansies and **violas** are invaluable for spring baskets, and the pansies, in particular, come in colours to suit everyone, from the most subtle to the brightest and cheeriest. Plant them in early spring and they'll put on a huge surge of growth as the weather warms up, flowering like mad right through to early summer.

One of the most delightful ways of punctuating this mass of flower, especially if you're working within the blue/violet colour range, is with the pretty button heads of **bellis daisies**. Their charm lies in their simplicity, and in their clear shades of white, rose and deep pink, the flowers produced in profusion right through spring.

Forget-me-nots, too, are naturals for spring baskets, adding a haze of bright blue flowers. The ordinary garden form is a bit wild and shaggy for baskets, but the relatively new 'Blue Ball' is especially compact, forming a dense globe to no more than 15cm/6in. Miniature white and pink forget-me-nots

are available too, and very pretty they are, but the traditional blue remains our favourite.

To create one of the great spring pictures of all time, add some yellow **primroses** to the forget-me-nots. This is one of the classic combinations – simple flowers in simple colours that breathe the cool freshness of spring woods and hedgerows – totally beguiling. Take care to use hardy primroses, rather than those that collapse in frost and are useful only for cool conservatories or porches. The ones to look for are the yellow forms of 'Wanda' hybrids, or the softer, more delicate yellow of our native primrose, *Primula vulgaris* which is one of the most exquisite of all spring flowers.

Finally, don't forget trailers such as **ivy**, and semi-trailers such as **ajuga** and **lamium**, in all their wonderful range of leaf colours, which are a good foil for many flowers. And, of course, **bulbs**. Use miniature daffodils like 'Tête-à-Tête' to make a golden topping to a basket, and to these you can add clumps of bright blue muscari (grape hyacinth) and the dangling heads of blue or white scilla.

Your spring-planted baskets may seem a short term investment, but it's a whole quarter of a year that you've filled with colour and interest.

Basket plants for beginners

If you've only just embarked on a colourful career in hanging baskets and you're feeling a bit nervous about it, take heart. First look at our easy-care basket (pages 24-5), which shows you all the easiest ways of making sure that your plants are kept well fed and watered. Then take advantage of all those docile, even-tempered plants that will give you an absolute minimum of bother.

Plants are like people – some take offence much more readily than others, particularly if you don't offer them a drink. This usually takes the form of drastic shrivelling and weeks of nursing them back to health. Fuchsias are especially good at this trick. What we need here are the plants that have a robust attitude to adversity. An almost Gallic, 'C'est la vie'

HANDLE WITH CARE

As we've shown, there's a very wide range of basket plants that can shrug off a period of neglect. But others can be much more temperamental, needing a constant supply of water to give of their best:

ferns	mimulus
fuchsia	nepeta/glechoma
hosta	pansies
lobelia	scaevola
lysimachia	tuberous begonia

---

stance. They mooch about, all Jean Paul Belmondo and leather-jacketed, dangling a Gauloise and shrugging off life's little problems.

The most remarkable of all drought-resistant plants is, happily, one of the best basket plants of all,

The geranium, with its remarkable resistance to drought, is the most easy-going of all basket plants.

the **geranium**, which can be deprived of water for weeks before they finally give up. They look pretty miserable through this process, so we don't recommend that you leave them unwatered for more than a few days, but they are tremendous survivors. And look at the choice you've got – a huge range of colours and a variety of shapes from the sturdy upright varieties that will top a basket beautifully, to the trailing ivy-leaved forms. Of these latter, you could fill a whole basket with just two or three plants of the vigorous 'continental' or 'balcon' geraniums. They shoot out masses of flowers, and make a quite spectacular display.

Bidens, with its feathery foliage and generous scatter of bright gold flowers is another easy-going character. If you leave it unwatered for a few days, it droops and looks sad, but very quickly perks up when watered again. And **nasturtiums** actually prefer a life on the dry side, evidenced by their ability to grow vigorously in any dry, sunny patch of ground. But don't put too many in a mixed basket – they've a habit of elbowing out the opposition. Two, or a maximum of three, will be manageable, especially if you use a bushy, rather than trailing, form.

Other good guys? In the flowering department, **brachycome**, **busy lizzie**, **convolvulus** and **felicia**, closely followed by **petunia** and **verbena**. These last two recover well after a dry period, but there's a catch – they are susceptible to powdery mildew, and the gardener-induced drought will make them all the more vulnerable.

For spring baskets, **bulbs** couldn't be easier. They're like little pre-programmed packages, containing all that's needed for guaranteed flowering, and the only thing they dislike is too much water, which is very unlikely in a hanging basket.

When it comes to foliage, there's little that will give you trouble. Small **shrubs** and **conifers** are exceedingly tough, **herbs** such as thyme and rosemary love a good dry roasting, and there are several trailing plants that can survive quite a degree of neglect. One of the very toughest and showiest is furry-leaved **helichrysum**, while **cineraria**, **plectranthus**, **ivy** (Hedera), **lamium** and the filigree silver **lotus** are also survivors.

BACKGROUND DETAILS

When you're planning the colours for your basket, don't forget the background against which it will be viewed. An all-white basket, for instance, is a lovely thing, but it's going to look pretty anaemic if you hang it against a white wall. Similarly, a red basket against a red brick wall will either disappear or clash horribly.

Use the basket to pick up on and echo any nearby colours. If, say, you're lucky enough to have honey-coloured Cotswold stone walls, highlight them with a mass of gold. Or put a basket of bright red geraniums and petunias next to a cherry red door. It's a simple trick, but the overall effect is very sophisticated.

Conversely, try to avoid arguments between neighbouring colours. You may, for instance, have a tub planted up with a soft pink scheme, above which hangs your basket. If the basket is full of vibrant reds and oranges, the two containers will sit very uneasily together.

The warm tones of this basket echo its red brick setting and make a strong contrast with the dark doorway.

BASKETS FOR SHADE

BASKETS FOR SHADE

HEAVY SHADE

Don't let shady corners cast you into a gloom. Give them a bright new outlook by hanging up a few baskets, where, a surprisingly wide range of plants will thrive. Take the worst-case scenario – a sunless angle between two walls for instance, or heavy shade cast by a tree. Even here, all is far from lost and you can grow displays every bit as pleasing as those you might grow in sun.

For wonderfully bright summer colour, there are two plants that will never let you down. First the marvellous **busy lizzies** (impatiens) which are neatly compact plants with a mass of summer-long flowers in a huge range of colours. Opt for light colours for a shady situation because they really stand out, though a bright colour such as red can also look good, quietly glowing like a fire in a darkened room.

Your other colourful allies in heavy shade are the fibrous-rooted **semperflorens begonias** – again, very compact, and they flower right through to the first frosts. Available in all shades of pink, white and red, some also have attractive bronze foliage. One of the prettiest in a shady spot is 'Olympia Starlet' (widely available from seed), which has bright green leaves and white flowers edged with rose pink, looking as fresh as apple blossom.

Two invaluable plants for shade. The sculpted leaves of hostas (top) for a cool, elegant feel, and the sheer exuberance of busy lizzies (above) with their enormous colour range.

Both of these look their best when massed in single colours in a basket, pouch or tower – a mix reduces their impact considerably. And because they're so uniformly compact, they're absolutely superb if you use them for a flower ball basket (see pages 34-5).

The other great plants for heavy shade don't have the same colour impact as busy lizzies and begonias, but you can create some very quiet, peaceful effects. Think of the beautiful picture that mosses and ferns make growing in a wood, then translate it to a basket. Moss it heavily, then plant up a few **ferns** (look out for evergreen varieties, which will be useful year-round), and young, small-leaved **hostas** like white-edged 'Ground Master'. If you keep the basket pretty moist, the plants will enjoy it and the moss will stay fresh and green, making a beautiful contrast of colours and textures.

For trailers to lighten the gloom, any of the **lamiums** will do a good job, particularly the white-splashed forms like 'White Nancy'. And **ivy** is incomparable. This remarkably versatile and tolerant plant will thrive in even the shadiest corner. For maximum impact, choose a variegated form. Yellow is especially good.

PARTIAL SHADE

What exactly do we mean by 'partial shade'? It's a wonderfully loose term, but to us it means a number of situations. It could be the dappled shade cast by an open-leaved tree like a birch; a position that receives just a few hours of sun each day; or a sunless north wall that is open to the sky and not heavily overshadowed by buildings or trees. It always amazes us just how wide a range of plants will grow happily in these conditions.

Prime amongst them are **fuchsias**, which drip with gorgeous blooms throughout summer. They're particularly suitable for shadier baskets because in sun they can dry out in a flash and take an age to recover, but in a shady spot, where there isn't the same drastic loss of moisture, they're much less vulnerable.

Fuchsias give soft, romantic colour, but if you want something rather more electrifying but just as longlasting – go for **tuberous begonias**. The colours can be remarkably bright, from sizzling orange to dazzling scarlet, and just two or three plants of the pendulous varieties will take over a whole basket in a cascade of flower. If you're not quite comfortable with such bold colours, there's also a range of much more muted pastel tones, including a delicious apricot shade.

Another plant that offers you a wide choice of colours for a shady spot is **mimulus**. Most widely

Frilly-skirted 'Swingtime' is just one of the hundreds of fuchsia varieties that will relish a position in partial shade, where they are much less prone to drying out.

available from seed, take your pick from a rich mix like 'Calypso' (velvety, spotted flowers in shades of orange), or something much subtler like 'Andean Nymph', a beautiful combination of ivory and blush-pink. But you must remember that their preferred habitat is the water's edge, so keep them thoroughly moist at all times.

Other good basket plants that will tolerate lower light levels include feathery, daisy-like **brachycome** and **felicia**, that invaluable filler **lobelia**, and two excellent trailers – **helichrysum** and **glechoma (nepeta)**. Most of the small evergreens that you use to top a basket will also do well, especially **euonymus**, whose gold-variegated forms shine out especially brightly in shade.

Spring bulbs are also great performers in shade, so tuck in plenty when you're planting in autumn – it's only tulips that really need sun. Smaller varieties of **daffodil**, like jaunty little 'Tête-à-Tête', look wonderful topping a basket, and fat clumps of snowdrops would look good around the rim. **Iris reticulata** is another dainty beauty for partial shade, and even **crocuses** will do well, although they won't open out quite so generously as they do in sun.

Along with the bulbs, add in some of those plants that put on a great burst of colour in mid to late spring when the weather warms up: **winter pansies** and **violas**, for instance (which will have given you some flower over winter), together with a haze of **forget-me-nots**, or the dense leaf rosettes and pretty flower clusters of the hardy 'Wanda' **primulas**.

The world may not be your oyster when it comes to basket gardening in shade, but there are still plenty of pearls to be had.

The electrically bright colours of tuberous begonias make a real impact in a shady spot.

GROWING FOOD IN HANGING BASKETS

Strawberry 'Temptation'.

GROWING FOOD IN HANGING BASKETS

We tend to think of summer baskets as flowery extravaganzas, but they can be equally decorative filled with tasty food crops.

Take **tomatoes** as an example. 'Tumbler' is a cascading variety especially bred for baskets. It produces plenty of fruit and has an excellent flavour. Unlike conventional tomatoes it needs no staking or pinching out, and it looks wonderful in a sunny spot, the clusters of small red fruits as tempting as dangling cherries. Add in some trailing blue lobelia or white busy lizzies and you've a very pretty picture indeed. Plant in your hanging basket when there's no longer any danger of frost, and once the first small fruits have set, feed weekly with liquid tomato food.

Because tomatoes need lots of water, grow them in a plastic pot rather than a wire basket which is much more vulnerable to drying out. If deprived of water the fruit can crack or develop 'blossom end rot' (which you can identify by blackened patches at the base of the fruit). One plant will easily fill a 35cm/14in pot and, the seedsmen tell us, can produce up to 4kg/9lbs of delicious tomatoes.

Strawberries are ideal for hanging baskets, relishing the good compost and are safely out of reach of slugs, snails and the woodlice that usually try to eat them. You can produce bumper crops in a sunny spot, especially in a pouch or flower tower, which will house several plants. In this situation, you can plan for a succession of fruit by planting up different varieties. Choose delicious 'Honeoye', for example, for early crops, 'Hapil' for mid-season flavour, and the new 'Calypso' for tasty crops from early summer right until the first frosts. For maximum yields, keep them evenly watered and feed once a week with liquid tomato food.

As for planting companions for these luscious fruits, don't forget that they need plenty of sun and air to do well, so stick to daintier varieties. Choose feathery-leaved brachycome or felicia, for instance, with their blue daisy flowers, or the shiny stars of white solenopsis for a 'strawberries and cream' basket.

HIGH-RISE HERBS

There's something very relaxing and peaceful about a herb garden; a kind of natural aromatherapy as the scents envelop you on a sunny day. So why not try the same thing in mid-air, especially if space on the ground is short. A herb basket in a sunny spot (ideally by the kitchen door) will be a delight – subtle colours, lovely leaf contrasts, and simple flowers that bees and butterflies will adore.

Of the herbs that you'll use in your cooking, creeping **thyme** is a beauty for a basket and gives you a good range of leaf colour and pretty summer flowers. **Golden marjoram** (*Origanum vulgare* 'Aureum'), with its small soft leaves, makes a stunning mat of fresh green-gold.

TIPS

✔ *Turn strawberry and tomato baskets now and again to ensure even, all-round growth and good fruit ripening.*

✔ *If there are still green, unripe fruits on your tomatoes when frosts threaten, pick whole branches and hang them upside down indoors – the goodness from the stem seems to speed ripening, so they won't be wasted.*

✔ *Strawberry plants eventually deteriorate with age, so you'll get much better crops if you start afresh every couple of years. Potted plants can be expensive, but mail order plants are very reasonable.*

Chives would look good in the top of the basket, where their mauve pompon flowers are an attractive bonus and can be added to salads along with the leaves.

Young plants of evergreen herbs like **sage**, **rosemary** and **bay** can also be used to top the basket, lasting for a couple of seasons before they get too big and bushy and have to be transferred to the garden. Look out for the variegated and purple-flushed sages, which are especially decorative.

Now you've chosen your cooking herbs, take advantage of all those plants that are classified as herbs because of their medicinal qualities. There's an astonishing number that qualify (from roses to heathers and even oak trees) and among them are some little beauties that fit very neatly into a hanging basket. One of the most ornamental is **nasturtium**, giving a cheery splash of gold, orange or red, its pepper-flavoured leaves and flowers adding zest to summer salads. The bright orange petals of **pot marigolds** can also look very pretty scattered over a mix of salad leaves.

Violas, too, have medicinal properties, so they're also legitimate occupants. *Viola tricolor* (the heartsease pansy) is an especially pretty little plant and can often be found in the wild flower section at the garden centre. And migraine sufferers will tell you just how effective are the leaves of **feverfew** (*Tanacetum parthenium*), which makes a bushy little mound of leaves and white daisy flowers.

Finally, try **alpine strawberries**, not simply because they're good for the skin and digestion, but because they're utterly charming. Neat leaves, tiny white flowers, and with small dangling fruits that are best eaten when deeply red and ripe.

With its domed habit, sage (top right) makes a tasty topping for a basket, and violas (above) are an ideal flowery infill.

SHADY CHARACTERS

Mint is an excellent plant for a large basket in a shady spot, where it can be kept moist and cool. The snag is that the thuggish roots will, in time, send out a mass of new stems and swamp daintier subjects – so best, we think, for a basket that's going to be dismantled at the end of the season. Team it up with parsley, which enjoys the same conditions and is best planted afresh each year, and with chives, which don't absolutely insist on a sunny position.

GROWING FOOD IN HANGING BASKETS

Window boxes

Window boxes are one of the best kept secrets in gardening; they are seldom seen, even in towns and other places where growing space is at a premium, and we felt this was a real shame. But, at last, their popularity is on the rise again, with a new generation of gardeners who have begun to discover that they're easier to care for and even more versatile than hanging baskets, so it won't be long before they're just as fashionable.

Window boxes are easier than hanging baskets in lots of ways. They are simple to plant up and because they hold a greater volume of compost than most hanging baskets, your plants will flourish because there's less competition for space. You also won't have to water them as frequently as baskets.

You can also grow a much wider range of plants, such as osteospermums and marguerites that would look top-heavy in a hanging basket, fuchsias that can be tricky in baskets because they hate to dry out, and small shrubs. So the opportunity for experimenting is even greater – which is why we enjoy it so much.

TIPS

✔ *When buying a terracotta window box, make sure it is frost proof (and do keep the receipt, as any damage usually shows up in the second or third winter).*

✔ *Wooden window boxes can be decorated to match your house colours, and very smart they look. Alternatively, if you are feeling especially creative, you could try stencilling, marbling or ragging. These lovely paint techniques can be found in any good painting and decorating book.*

✔ *Fibreglass window boxes are sold at some garden centres and occasionally through mail order suppliers. They are expensive, but will last for many years. Imitation lead boxes are especially grand and look glorious in a traditional setting.*

Terracotta boxes, lined up and ready to go, packed with instant colour. But they will need to be fixed very securely in position; their weight makes them pretty lethal if they fall.

Basic equipment

CHOOSING YOUR WINDOW BOX

Window boxes are generally sold in metric lengths of 40, 60, 80 and 100cm, so first measure up your windowsill. If it's over 100cm, you will have to use two boxes, but these can be disguised either with trailing plants or by placing the boxes in an outer wooden sleeve so that it looks like one box (see our step-by-step guide on pages 56-7). We think that window boxes on sills tend to look best if they almost fill the window recess, but those mounted below the sill look better if they are slightly shorter than the sill, so bear this in mind when measuring your space.

When it comes to the width and depth of the box, the bigger the better, so long as the width fits the available space – a width and depth of 20cm/8in is ideal. Bigger boxes hold more compost so don't need watering as frequently. They can also accommodate larger plants, which is handy if you're planting for instant effect.

The most widely available boxes are made from **plastic**, and the better quality models are tough and long-lasting (cheaper boxes are a false economy because they soon become brittle in sunlight and are easily broken). Pick a model with a good solid rim, which makes the box easier to hold when planted up and less likely to split if dropped or handled awkwardly.

The basic models are relatively utilitarian, in green, brown or white, and although the manufacturers undoubtedly regard them as objects of beauty, the plastic can look shiny and stark. A wooden sleeve can be used to provide a much more attractive finish.

More stylish (and more expensive) models are also available. Some are elegantly raised on small feet, and are stable so long as your windowsill is flat, and others are crafted to resemble terracotta; the better quality 'terracotta' boxes really do look as good as the real thing, yet are not as heavy. To make life easier, you can even buy a range of self-watering models that have built-in reservoirs.

You'll also find a tempting range of genuine **terracotta** boxes, which are extremely handsome and

Terracotta has tremendous charm, its warm, earthy tones growing ever richer and more mellow over the years.

look even better as they age and mellow. Some are plain, with just a bit of fluting, while others are wonderfully ornamental (and, of course, wonderfully expensive). But try to avoid the smaller models (anything under 20cm/8in wide and deep) – the small volume of compost together with the natural porosity of the clay means that they dry out very quickly. Incidentally, the biggest terracotta boxes are immensely heavy, especially when planted up, so it's best to use them on windowsills rather than under the sill because most brackets wouldn't be strong enough to cope with the weight.

Wood window boxes are more difficult to find and can be expensive, though anyone with the slightest DIY skill should be able to make their own. The major problem with wooden boxes is that they slowly deteriorate over the years as moisture from the compost seeps into the wood. To delay the process, treat the interior with a bituminous paint, or line with polythene.

For a cheap and cheerful window box you can't beat the **compressed fibre** boxes that look a bit like dark brown papier mâché; if you don't like the look, you can always hide them in an outer wooden sleeve in the same way as plastic boxes. But cheapness comes at a price, and because they're biodegradable, they're unlikely to last for more than a season.

WINDOW BOX FIXINGS

Window boxes can be extremely heavy so it's essential to secure them properly – we've heard horrific stories of boxes falling and hurting people or damaging property. So please don't take the risk; take a few moments to make sure your box is safe. And do it before you plant up; full boxes make the job twice as difficult.

...FOR BOXES ON WINDOWSILLS

Most windowsills slope slightly, so place a couple of chocks under the box to level it. This not only helps prevent the box from slipping off but also lets water drain away more easily.

Next, using a couple of angle brackets, fix the box to the side of the window or, if it's easier, fix it to the sill. Alternatively, screw a couple of eye hooks into the wooden window frame, then drill a 3mm/⅛in hole through each end of the back of the box. Galvanised

wire threaded between the eye hooks and holes will keep the box firmly in place. If your window frames are metal or plastic, secure the eye hooks to the wall instead, using the appropriate wall plugs.

...FOR BOXES BENEATH WINDOWSILLS

Garden centres sell special brackets to support window boxes, with a lip that prevents the box from slipping off. The alternative is to use heavy-duty hanging basket brackets, fixed in place with plugs and screws. To prevent the box from sliding forward, drill a couple of holes in the back of the box and screw it into the wall.

When you're positioning the brackets, aim to get the top of the box at least 5cm/2in or so below the window ledge – any closer and you might block the drip channel on the underside of most sills. But if you have side-opening windows, or you're growing especially tall plants that could take light from the room, lower the box even further.

The brackets should be positioned so that the weight of the box is evenly distributed, leaving an overlap of 10cm/4in or so at each end. As an extra precaution, attach the box to the brackets with galvanised wire.

...FOR BOXES ON RAILINGS

You can buy special brackets which hook onto railings and hold the box safely and securely.

COMPOST AND EXTRAS

As we stressed with hanging baskets, it's important to buy a good compost. Garden soil, however good it looks, won't drain well, and may be harboring pests and diseases. For bedding plants, summer bulbs and vegetables, multipurpose compost is fine, or even the decanted contents of a growbag. For herbs, spring-flowering bulbs and any permanent plants such as shrubs or conifers, we prefer the more gutsy John Innes No 2 loam-based compost. But it's not too critical which you use – the important thing is that it's decent compost rather than garden soil.

If you're planting a summer window box, it's well worth incorporating water retention granules into the compost, together with some slow release fertiliser (see page 15). Anything for an easy life!

Whatever type of box you use, security is paramount; they should be very firmly anchored in position, with no possibility of them slipping and falling.

Making a stylish window box sleeve

This handsome design was created by Ian Scot, and is easily adaptable to any size of windowsill. It's a sleeve rather than a solid box, so it is ideal for disguising plain plastic boxes, and because the wood isn't in direct contact with the soil, it should last for years.

The front of the box is angled forward, to match the shape of the two troughs that it surrounds, but it would be easy to adapt the design to fit a rectangular trough. To estimate the amount of wood you will need, measure your existing trough and add an inch all round (so that, for instance, a 20cm/8in side becomes a 25cm/10in side). This allows room for the inner battens, and prevents you from trapping your fingers when you place the trough inside the sleeve.

Ready-made wooden sleeves can be pretty expensive, so it's worth honing your DIY skills to create a sleeve that's both stylish and cost-effective.

HARDWARE
exterior grade 25cm/10in plywood
planed Iroko, 5cm x 0.5cm/2in x ¼in
angle beading
zinc-plated screws
copper nails
waterproof wood glue
copper panel pins
preservative or varnish

ESSENTIAL TOOLS
saw
drill
screwdriver
spirit level
hammer
tape

USEFUL TOOLS
mitre box
battery screwdriver

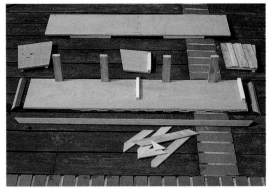

1 Cut all the timber to size. In this design the front panel slopes forward, so the side and centre panels are cut square on the back edge and at an angle on the front.

2 Glue two battens to a side panel then attach it to the back panel with two countersunk screws. Do the same to fix the central strut.

3 Attach the other end in the same way, then screw a piece of batten along the top and bottom to act as buffers between box and wall. Fix the front panel.

4 Use two screws to securely fix each end of the four bottom supports. These give the box extra strength to take the weight of the planted up window boxes.

6 Add strips of hardwood beading, cut with a mitre box at 45 degrees at the corners (or ask your local hardware store to do this). This prevents water from seeping between the cladding strips.

5 Use a spacer to check that the pattern of the iroko cladding is consistent. The front cladding is set at a 45 degree angle, when glued and pinned.

7 Paint or varnish the box and let it dry. Mark the centre of the windowsill. Make sure the box is level and fix securely into position with long screws.

8 The finished sleeve, with its planted troughs, makes a stylish and long-lasting feature for any window.

Growing success

Growing success with window boxes is virtually guaranteed, because what you're dealing with is essentially a very large, rectangular pot. Once you've provided it with good drainage, filled it with fresh compost and completed the easy task of planting up, you'll find that aftercare is pretty simple. So, if you haven't tried your hand at window box gardening before, give it a go. It's very straightforward, and a lovely way to put flowers in the frame.

Perfect symmetry in a box that couldn't be easier to care for – just trim up the box (Buxus) *hedge now and again, and replace the bedding plants according to the season.*

CHOOSING YOUR PLANTS

We've always found it more challenging choosing plants for window boxes than for hanging baskets. Baskets are relatively straightforward; you need height in the centre and an assortment of smaller and trailing plants around the edge. But with window boxes there is far more opportunity to be creative.

It's not just a matter of heights and spreads, it's also the shapes of the plants that will influence the look of the display. You might, for instance, decide on a planting with the highest point in the centre, then slowly tier down with medium height domes of tuberous begonias, for example, placing small plants at each end. Edge with some trailers like verbena and the picture is complete. Or you could change the balance entirely by using the same range of plants in a different configuration – a tall fuchsia at each end, a single tuberous begonia in the centre and an infill of busy lizzies and verbena.

Both these boxes will have a gently rounded outline made up of a series of bushy domes, but you might want to incorporate a few spikier plants to make an interesting contrast. Cordylines do a good job here, forming an explosive fountain of leaves which are especially attractive in the red-variegated forms. Conifers are useful, too, especially if you use a columnar variety like the grey-green *Juniperus Communis* 'Compressa' – great as a centrepiece, or to stand sentinel at each end of the box. For a window box that will be placed in shade, hostas are real beauties, and you'll find many narrow-leaved forms like white-edged 'Ground Master', which will be ideal. Or you could opt for edible spikes – chives

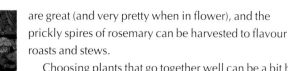

CHOOSING YOUR PLANTS

are great (and very pretty when in flower), and the prickly spires of rosemary can be harvested to flavour roasts and stews.

Choosing plants that go together well can be a bit hit-and-miss unless you're already very familiar with them, but there are several ways of putting together a window box scheme that's guaranteed to succeed:

● Take a look at some local window boxes – the neighbours might have hit on a winning formula, and many pubs and offices put on stunning displays. And you can also see what doesn't work...

● Mail order seedsmen and nurseries now offer an excellent range of plug plants for summer displays, and many also supply them in carefully themed 'collections'. These are invaluable in our experience, with the colour illustrations accurately reflecting the results that you can achieve.

● If you're planting your window box in May, you'll find plenty of well-grown plants, many already in flower, at the garden centre. It's easy enough to take your window box along (or borrow one when you get there) and simply gather up the plants that take your eye. Shuffle them around in the box, discard those that don't suit and replace them with those that do, until you're happy with the combination. Obviously the plants will grow larger in time, but this technique will give you a pretty good idea of how the box will look over the coming months.

As with hanging baskets, it's important to select good quality plants. However large or small they are, there should be an air of good health about them – the plant sturdy and compact, and the leaves a good colour with no sign of yellowing or spotting. Wilted, pot-bound or spindly plants have had a chequered past, and are best left at the garden centre.

PLANTING UP

As you can see from our step-by-step sequence on pages 62-3, planting up a window box is a quick and simple task. There are just 3 essential things to remember:

● A drainage layer is essential to prevent compost from washing through the drainage holes or even blocking them. Coarse grit is fine but you could equally well use gravel, Hortag expanded clay granules or even a layer of small stones from the garden.

● Do use a good compost. For bedding plants and other annuals choose a multipurpose compost, but if you want to grow perennials like box (*Buxus*) , you'll be better off using the more substantial loam-based John

Innes No. 2. If you've decided to feed your plants with slow release fertiliser, mix the granules into the compost before planting up.

● It's important to water plants thoroughly an hour or so before planting. If they're planted dry, it's possible for the rootball to remain dry even when the surrounding compost is thoroughly soaked.

AFTERCARE

Watering is the most time-consuming task in caring for window boxes, especially in a long, hot summer. Happily, though, they retain much more moisture than hanging baskets and even in the hottest weather a daily watering (morning or evening) should be sufficient. Incorporating water crystals into the compost before planting will help too – they store water and release it when the plants need it. The manufacturers claim that they can cut watering by up to half, and though we haven't done any scientific investigation into this, they certainly do seem to help. We wouldn't recommend them for winter window boxes, which need very little additional water. You only need to water them once a fortnight, and even then only if it doesn't rain.

The other routine tasks are feeding and dead-heading, and these we've covered on pages 20-21.

Regular dead-heading is important, to keep boxes looking neat and to keep them in full flower production.

CARING FOR WINDOW BOX PERENNIALS

If you've opted for the low maintenance route and planted up plenty of perennials in your window box, then they'll need a little care to keep them looking good from year to year.

Evergreens (with the exception of conifers) are bound to need the occasional prune, to keep them to a manageable size, to encourage fresh new growth, and to keep the more formal plants like box and *Lonicera nitida* looking crisp and smart. The actual method of pruning varies from plant to plant, but it's not as complex, or as time-consuming, as it might seem.

For the evergreens that we grow for their flowers, like pernettya, pieris and heathers, the best time to prune is directly after flowering to give the plant a chance to catch its breath for the following year. For the rest of the evergreens, spring is fine – the warming weather will encourage lots of healthy new growth in double-quick time. Any evergreens that you're growing as tightly clipped and formal, such as box (*Buxus*) may need a couple of trims through summer too. The only time that you really should keep the secateurs firmly clamped in their holster is autumn. The logic here is that by pruning when there's still some mild weather around, you encourage fresh new

Perennial plants are tremendously labour-saving, needing a minimum of routine care to keep them looking good.

growth that is going to be very susceptible to the first of the winter frosts.

And how severely should you prune? Let the habit of the plant be your guide. Plants like euonymus, santolina and box have a domed habit, so just clip them back all over by around a third. More 'stemmy' plants like pieris and pernettya can be trimmed back in the same way, to keep them compact, and they'll also benefit from the complete removal of up to a third of the older stems every two or three years, to encourage strong new growth from the base. To keep trailing ivy in good shape, cut back longer stems by half, and completely cut out any older, woodier stems that are looking tired and dusty.

For clump-forming, herbaceous plants like hosta, ajuga, heuchera and spreading alpines that can become overcrowded, divide them up every few years in late autumn or early spring. Just dig them up and separate them out into individual portions (easy enough with most plants, but others, like hosta, form a densely-knit root system and some damage is inevitable). Pick out the strongest, healthiest plantlets and replant, watering them well and keeping them watered through any dry spells.

Our 'can't-fail' window box

If your window boxes have been empty over the winter and you're itching for some spring colour, this is the window box for you. Plant this in late February, and use good-sized plants for instant impact. It will only take about 15 minutes to put together, and you will be rewarded with colour right through to the end of spring. The pansies bush out and flower with such eager-to-please exuberance that it will seem a crime to scrap them in favour of summer planting schemes.

This window box was designed for a very sheltered spot, so we used ordinary primula hybrids, but if you are planning to position your window box in a more exposed area, it would be wiser to use hardy 'Wanda' primulas (if they're not labelled, look for a bronze tinge to the leaves), or the simple wild primrose, *Primula vulgaris*.

It may seem expensive, buying all these plants just for a three-month display, but remember that you can keep the skimmia, ivy and lamium as permanent residents and use them as a foil for summer bedding plants. Or, if you have a garden, it's easy enough to transplant them and grow them on from year to year; the skimmia will eventually form a handsome large bush, the ivy could clothe a wall, and this particular lamium makes splendid, non-invasive ground cover.

HARDWARE
60cm/2ft window box
coarse grit or small stones
multipurpose compost (not shown)

PLANTS
1 x skimmia 'Rubella'
2 x narcissus 'Tête-à-Tête'
3 x winter pansy
2 x primula hybrids
2 x lamium 'White Nancy'
2 x ivy (hedera) 'Green Ripple'

It's easy to devise spring schemes like this because all the plants are in full flower when you pick them at the garden centre.

1 Make holes in the base of the box if necessary, spacing them approximately 7.5cm/3in apart. In a box this size, six holes would be sufficient.

2 Line the box with coarse grit or small stones to a depth of 2.5cm/1in to aid drainage, then top up with compost to the halfway mark.

3 Firm the compost down, then arrange the plants on top of it, to check their final planting position. Be sure to arrange them symmetrically to achieve a 'mirror image' effect.

4 Remove the pots and add more compost to fill around the plants, packing down gently but firmly. Water the window box well and top up any dips in the soil that may appear.

5 The finished box, looking very pretty and ready to give many weeks of colour. The dwarf narcissi, inevitably, will fade, but the winter pansies will bush out to fill the gap.

Planting ideas

Keep your window boxes in full production – they give terrific scope for summer colour, and even for a good range of fruit and vegetables, but they can also be used for some splendid winter schemes. At a relatively cheerless time of year (horticulturally speaking), these are doubly welcome.

SUMMER COLOUR

Summer is a time for spectacle and colour from the wondrous range of bedding plants offered by garden centres, seedsmen and mail order plant suppliers. They're only too eager to grow, and it's a joy to watch them reach their full potential, spurred on by summer heat and your careful watering and feeding.

So use them generously in your window boxes, to create a tumbling mass of flower and foliage that will last right through to the first frosts. Whether you've stuck to a tried and tested scheme or experimented with a bold new combination of plants and colours, a fully planted summer box is an absolute delight.

MAXIMUM IMPACT, MINIMUM EFFORT

A simple scheme is always best, and at its most basic you'll find that you can create some wonderful displays by planting one variety and colour. For example, a window box filled only with red 'balcon' geraniums is

Balance, harmony and impact – even the simplest of schemes can pack quite a punch, like this one-variety box filled with bright red geraniums.

an awesome sight throughout summer; a waterfall of colour created by thousands of flowers. It's got balance, harmony and impact – all the qualities you look for in a window box display, yet the planting scheme couldn't be easier.

We've seen other single plant schemes that have been just as impressive. A sea of pure white marguerites in a pale blue box; a terracotta box packed with the drama of dark-leaved, New Guinea hybrid busy lizzies which were covered in rosy pink flowers, and elsewhere a shady spot lit up by a box filled with bright yellow tuberous begonias. But whatever colour you choose – it's going to look terrific. Single planting is bold, beautiful and simple.

BOXING CLEVER WITH A VARIETY OF PLANTS

But you may want to be a little more adventurous – after all, one of the joys of window box gardening is the range of plants that can be grown in them, including some of the finest summer bedding plants like tobacco plant (nicotiana) and osteospermum which are far too big for hanging baskets but are perfect in window boxes.

So expand your single plant theme by adding in plants which will provide some contrast. And this is where the fun begins. You could use something that is a different colour of leaf or flower, or perhaps a different shape, but don't get too carried away – too many contrasts can create confusion and simple combinations are always the most effective.

Take a window box filled with marguerites for example. Tall and bushy, they would look wonderful fronted by small mounds of pale pink petunias. A few felted, silver helichrysum to trail over the edge of the box and the picture is complete. Being plantaholics, we know all too well the temptation to pop in even more plants – a geranium or two and perhaps a gorgeous new diascia. That's fine, but don't make it too much of a mix or you'll dilute the overall effect.

A stylish white planting with full, lush geranium blooms, tuberous begonias and lobelia.

It's the same with colour, too. The display will have far more impact if you don't mix too many different colours together. Simple, harmonious combinations like pink, blue, white and silver look very pretty. Try the lovely tobacco plant (nicotiana) 'Domino Salmon Pink' at the back of the box, with an underplanting of pure white busy lizzies and filmy-leaved, blue-flowered Swan River daisies. Or base the scheme around those reliable mainstays, geraniums and fuchsias, which provide some of the loveliest of pastel colours.

Bolder colour combinations work equally well. We're especially fond of blue and yellow which have the most extraordinary complementary effect on each other. Lemon yellow marguerites or osteospermums mixed with china-blue petunias and golden-leaved *Helichrysum* 'Limelight' is a potent and cheering mix. Or for a 'night sky' sort of picture, try a dark blue petunia like 'Midnight' as a backing for the bushy trails and gold stars of bidens.

For even richer colour, you'll find that strong vivid pinks and blues work extremely well together, and we were delighted with a dramatic violet and red scheme that we concocted, using 'Million Bells' petunias, geraniums and verbenas. We got the idea for it while experimenting at the garden centre, picking out plants and swapping them round until we achieved a happy colour combination.

Putting your colour scheme together at the garden centre is often the easiest way to hit on a really good mix of colours, so give it a try. Use our suggestions as a basis, by all means, but follow your own instincts too, trying new plants and ideas. Whatever you finally choose you're unlikely to go far wrong.

Careful colour theming in a bonfire blaze of yellow, red and orange (right) and a richly dramatic mix of purple and pink (below).

PLANTING FOR SCENT

A window box display is inevitably less interesting when viewed from inside the house, with most of the flowers turning their backs on you, and the tallest plants of a tiered arrangement obscuring your view of those at the front. The other problem is that strong daylight tends to throw the plants into silhouette so that they rarely look their best. That's why we're so keen on growing scented plants in boxes – if you can't enjoy the full beauty of the plants from the indoor perspective, at least you have the compensation of the delicious perfume that wafts into the room.

For summer schemes, there's a wealth of plants to choose from. Some, like herbs and scented-leaf geraniums, have aromatic leaves that release their perfumes when you brush a hand over them. Others charm our noses with their flowers and of these, **heliotrope** is one of the most desirable. The clusters of small, violet-blue flowers have an alluring almond scent, verging on cherry, which gives rise to its common name of 'cherry pie'. It grows to 35cm/14in or so, and with its attractive dark, almost bronze leaves, it makes a fine centrepiece for larger boxes.

Stocks (*Matthiola*) are also renowned for their rich, clove-like scent, and there's a very pretty dwarf strain called 'Cinderella' that reaches no more than 25cm/10in. The display is relatively short compared to other bedding plants, but you only need a few plants to release generous waves of perfume through June and July. **Verbenas** can be relied on for colour throughout summer, and they have a warm, spicy perfume that's especially strong in the evening. Richest of all, though, are blue and purple petunias, with a wonderful lily fragrance – marvellous.

In spring, some of the sweetest perfumes are provided by bulbs. As early as February, the delightful *Iris reticulata* cultivars burst into diminutive flower, with a scent redolent of sweet violets. They are soon followed by the dwarf forms of **narcissi** that are wonderful for window boxes, but pick them carefully – not all are scented. Four of the best are creamy-white, lemon-cupped 'Minnow', buttercup-yellow 'Baby Moon', golden-double 'Pencrebar' and gold, twin-headed 'Quail'. The perfume is especially sweet and fresh.

And when choosing plants for scent, you must, of course, include **hyacinths**. They have a delicious honey fragrance which is powerful enough to perfume the whole house. Their stiff, upright column of flowers suits formal plantings, and they always look their best if you grow one variety rather than mixing the colours.

Open the window on warmer days and let the pervasive fragrance of hyacinths waft in.

The bright berries of Solanum capsicastrum *bring cheer to boxes in milder areas.*

WINTER WARMERS

Although we love the flamboyance of summer displays, winter window boxes can also be very beautiful. Planted in autumn, just as the weather turns cold and the garden fizzles out like a damp squib as it prepares for hibernation, they're a ray of sunshine in a bleak world.

When we're putting box schemes together, we find it easiest to choose the bigger plants first – they're the vital structure, the evergreen backdrop around which you can work everything else. A plant like *Skimmia japonica* 'Rubella' is perfect. It forms a rounded bush with dark glossy leaves that develop an attractive reddish tint in winter. Buy it in bud, the bronze red clusters looking pretty throughout winter, and in spring the buds open to reveal pink, sweetly-scented flowers.

Pieris is another show stopper and the white-variegated forms like 'Flaming Silver' provide winter interest followed by a spring display of bright crimson new leaves. But if gold is more to your liking (and it does work especially well in winter), use bold-leaved, gold-variegated laurels (*Aucuba*), the smaller and more discreet *Euonymus* 'Emerald 'n' Gold' or the greeny-gold *Lonicera* 'Baggesen's Gold'.

Structure can be provided in other ways too. Rounded or pyramid dwarf conifers give a more formal touch, with a good choice of colours from bright green through steely blue to burnished gold. They look especially effective if you use them symmetrically rather than scattering them about – a matching pair at each end of the box, say, or one placed in the centre.

Dwarf box is another good choice and while the clipped forms are expensive, they add real style to any window box. One of the most attractive boxes we've ever seen consisted of a year-round, box mini-hedge,

fronted by seasonal colour like 'Miracle' cyclamen, and the finishing touch was a swag of variegated ivy sweeping round the front. This ivy was actually two plants, one at each end of the box, joined together in a loop when the plants had grown long enough.

Once the large plants are in place, add the highlights; the splashes of seasonal colour from plants like heathers, ornamental cabbages and winter pansies. And remember to pop in some bulbs while you're planting – snowdrops, *Iris reticulata* and specie crocus for the earliest flowers, and dwarf narcissi or rockery tulips for later colour. Finally, plant some ivy to trail over the side. It's the perfect plant for winter boxes, and you can choose colours from plain green to gold- and white-variegated to suit your colour scheme. It's also incredibly tough and, because it's perennial, can be used again when it's time to plant up your summer boxes.

Skimmia *'Rubella' retains its bronze buds through winter.*

The delicate markings of Iris reticulata *are a delight.*

GROWING FOOD IN WINDOW BOXES

Growing food in window boxes

Recent statistics suggest that less than a quarter of gardeners grow vegetables, which is an enormous shame because home-grown vegetables have unbeatable freshness and flavour. So let's redress the balance. There are over a dozen varieties of fruit and vegetables that will happily grow in window boxes, and every year the breeders help us out by introducing ever-smaller 'mini' varieties like the 30cm/12in aubergine plant 'Bambino'. A window box will never produce surplus crops for the freezer, but if you don't have a garden it's a wonderful way to savour that fresh-picked flavour.

For best results you'll need a sunny spot and a reasonably large window box – at least 20cm/8in deep and wide. This will hold sufficient compost for a wide range of crops – anything from the tangiest of tomatoes to the hottest of chilli peppers. This table lists the crops we would recommend as easy to grow, together with sowing times, and 'Best Edibles' on pages 98-101 discusses the very best, smaller varieties to opt for.

For the most part, the charm of growing fruit and vegetables lies in the anticipation of eating them, rather than in their looks. But there's no reason why you can't enhance the display by adding some trailing lobelia or 'Million Bells' petunias at the edge of the box. Real foodies might prefer to add some dwarf nasturtiums, because you can eat the peppery leaves and flowers.

There are, however, two cropping plants that are so pretty that they'd be at home in any floral display. 'Lollo Rossa' lettuce has beautiful frilly leaves which are tinged red, and the form of leaf beet called 'Rhubarb Chard' is also a real eye-catcher. The dark green, glossy leaves look (and taste) like spinach, but it's the leaf stalks that are so incredibly striking – a bright red that's so intense it almost glows. Pick the leaves regularly to encourage new growth and cook the green portion like spinach, and the stalks like asparagus. You are getting two vegetables for the price of one – terrific value!

CROP

AUBERGINE (mini)

BEANS, FRENCH

BEETROOT

CARROT

LEAF BEET (chard/Swiss chard)

LETTUCE

RADISH

SPRING ONION

STRAWBERRIES

SWEET PEPPER (mini)

TOMATOES

A box filled with edibles makes an interesting contrast of colours and shapes, together with the happy anticipation of harvesting ultra-fresh crops.

OWING/PLANTING TIME	SPACING	HARVEST	COMMENTS
ow in early spring, two seeds to a 9cm/3½ in pot. Place in a eated propagator or airing cupboard until germinated. emove the weaker seedling from each pot. Grow indoors warm, light conditions, and then plant outside when all anger of frost has passed.	20cm/8in	late summer	Must have a sheltered position, in full sun. Protect with horticultural fleece if early summer nights are unseasonably cold.
ow in early spring, two seeds to a 9cm/3½ in pot. Place in a eated propagator or airing cupboard until germinated. emove the weaker seedling from each pot. Grow indoors warm, light conditions, and then plant outside when all anger of frost has passed.	15cm/6in	2 months from planting. Pick regularly to keep them cropping.	Young plants are readily available at garden centres if you do not wish to grow from seed.
w directly into the box from mid-spring to midsummer.	5cm/2in Remove any surplus seedlings.	9 weeks from sowing. Harvest when 4cm/1½ in diameter.	Mini varieties (up to the size of a golf ball) are available.
w directly into the box from mid-spring to midsummer.	2.5cm/1in Remove any surplus seedlings.	2 months from sowing. Start harvesting when 2.5cm/1in in diameter.	Short, rounded carrots like 'Early French Frame' or 'Parmex' and finger carrots such as 'Suko' are by far the best varieties for window box cultivation.
w directly into the box in late spring. Alternatively, w indoors in early spring at room temperature, grow on individual pots in a warm, light room and plant out in te spring.	20cm/8in	2 months from sowing. Pick young leaves regularly.	If left in the box over winter, will start growing again in early spring.
w directly into the box between early spring and idsummer.	15cm/6in Remove surplus seedlings.	2 months after sowing. Pick young leaves of looseleaf varieties such as 'Lollo Rossa' regularly, harvest others when a good 'heart' has formed.	Will tolerate partial shade. Keep well watered in hot weather. In a sunny position, looseleaf varieties are less likely to 'bolt' (flower and die) than others.
w directly into the box in early spring.	2.5cm/1in Remove surplus seedlings.	4-6 weeks	Matures so rapidly that several crops can be sown in succession. Especially useful as a 'catch crop' between other vegetables early in the year.
w directly into the box anytime between early spring and idsummer.	2.5cm/1in Remove surplus seedlings.	6-8 weeks	Useful early crop. Keep well watered in dry weather.
ant out in spring for crops in the same year, or in autumn r crops the following year.	15cm/6in	summer to autumn	Must have full sun for good ripening. A mix of varieties (early, mid and late) will provide you with strawberries from early summer to mid autumn.
w in early spring, two seeds to a 9cm/3½ in pot. Place in a eated propagator or airing cupboard until germinated. emove the weaker seedling from each pot. Grow indoors warm, light conditions, and then plant outside when all anger of frost has passed.	20cm/8in	late summer	Must have a warm, sheltered position, in full sun.
w in late winter to early spring, two seeds to a 9cm/3½ in t. Place in a heated propagator or airing cupboard until rminated. Remove the weaker seedling from each pot. row indoors in warm, light conditions, and then plant utside when all danger of frost has passed.	30cm/12in	late summer	Most tomatoes are far too rampant for window boxes, but compact 'Tumbler' is ideal, producing good crops of small, tasty fruit.

Keeping the costs down

Planting up hanging baskets and window boxes can be a costly business, but with a little forward planning it's perfectly possible to have a superb show for remarkably little money.

THINKING BIG

The simplest way of achieving an outstanding hanging basket or window box at minimal cost is to think BIG. You have to think of all the plants that don't know when to stop growing and flowering, so that each individual plant fills the whole basket or box.

Take 'Surfinia' **petunias** as a prime example. By midsummer, just three plants in a large basket will be a massive explosion of flower, trailing and bushing to 1.2m/4ft or more. And they are available in a terrific range of colours, from bright white, through pinks and magentas to deep violet-blue. The 'Wave' series (available from seed), is equally vigorous, and though they're currently only available in a limited range of colours, no doubt by the time you read this the breeders will have come up with more.

Another good value plant is **bidens**, its dainty gold flowers and feathery foliage belying its toughness and vigour. It's a free-flowering bushy trailer, easily reaching 60cm/2ft or more in double-quick time.

Fuchsias, too, are great value for money, forming a dense cover that can be as much as 60cm/2ft wide and (in the case of the trailing varieties) deep. Put three plants in a 90cm/3ft window box and you won't need to add anything else.

Most **geraniums** won't grow large enough to fill a whole hanging basket or window box, but the trailing

Tough and trouble-free, bidens grows at an amazing rate, flowering all summer long.

continental or 'balcon' varieties are the exception. They send out great starbust sprays of flower and can trail to 90cm/3ft – like the fuchsias, three plants is an ample sufficiency for one basket or box.

For really vigorous foliage, look no further than **plectranthus** (white-variegated and incredibly bushy, trailing to 60cm/2ft or more), and **helichrysum** with its arching, spreading habit and attractive, felted leaves of silver or lime green. We once let it loose in a full size half-barrel, and it completely took over. With the more limited amount of compost in a window box or hanging basket, it won't achieve quite these proportions, but you'll certainly never need more than one or two plants to make a fantastic impact.

GROWING FROM SEED

Brachycome 'Strawberry mousse'

It's not difficult either, and you can achieve wonderful summer bedding plant displays in which the major investment has been simply your own time and patience. (Vegetables can be grown from seed, of course, but they don't need all the heat that most bedding plants require for germination. You'll find a run-down of the various methods of growing them in our table on pages 70-71.)

GROWING FROM SEED

Growing from seed is tremendously satisfying – there's the thrill of achievement, and the happy glow of knowing that it cuts your costs dramatically. Just have a browse through those seed catalogues that list the approximate number of seeds in each packet, and you'll be amazed at the difference in price between seeds and plug plants.

TIPS

✔ *Some seed is incredibly tiny, and virtually impossible to handle (it sticks to your fingers) or to sow evenly. To overcome this, mix it with a teaspoon or so of silver sand, shake to mix thoroughly, then gently trickle the mix over the compost.*

✔ *Seedlings are ultra-susceptible to disease, so always wash out pots and trays before sowing.*

✔ *Rather than covering newly sown seeds with compost, try using vermiculite. These light, white granules seem to retain warmth and moisture especially well, and we've had really good results with them. They are widely available and inexpensive.*

✔ *If you're averse to the admittedly fiddly process of pricking out small seedlings, grow them in small modules or 'plugs' instead. Sow two seeds per module, remove the smaller of the two germinated seedlings and leave the remaining seedlings to grow on until the roots have filled the compost, then pop out the whole plug and plant it up.*

SOWING

It's important, first of all, to use a decent seed and cutting compost. This provides the good drainage that seedlings need, and has just the right amount of fertiliser for the tender young roots. Firm it down into your chosen pot or seed tray, but don't compact it so much that the roots will struggle to grow.

Let the seed packet be your guide on when to sow, though in our experience early spring is fine for most plants – any earlier and they can struggle in the low light levels at that time of year. Take careful note, too, of the sowing depth – it can be crucial to success, and some seeds don't need to be covered at all. Scatter the seed as evenly as possible over the pot or tray (larger seeds can be set at neat intervals), and cover with more compost as necessary. Water from a watering can with a fine rose (a jet of water will disturb the soil), or by standing the pot or tray in water – the compost should be evenly moist but not soggy.

GERMINATING

Bedding plants can need temperatures of anything between 15-24°C/60-75°F for successful germination and, again, the seed packet will tell you. If you have an airing cupboard, or a shelf above a central heating boiler, that should do the trick for the vast majority of plants. Just seal the pots or trays inside a polythene bag or cover with clingfilm and keep an eye on them regularly to check for germination.

If you don't have a useful heat source, then a heated propagator is the answer. The simpler models are relatively cheap, and suit a wide range of plants. Those with thermostats can be expensive, but they're useful for

plants like geraniums, which demand higher temperatures, and for very fine seeds, such as begonias, that need very specific temperatures for good germination. All you do is place the pots inside the propagator and adjust the vents occasionally to clear any build-up of moisture on the inside of the lid. The seeds do the rest.

POTTING ON

Once a good forest of seedlings has appeared, remove the pots or trays from the heat source (and remove any covers), and place on a bright windowsill (away from direct sun) in a warm room. Keep the seedlings gently watered until they're large enough for pricking out – usually when the second set of leaves has appeared. Smaller seedlings can be pricked out into trays or individual small modules, larger seedlings into individual 9cm/3½in pots filled with any good multipurpose compost.

Nemesias (top) are very easy to grow from seed. Young seedlings can be pricked out into seed trays (above).

The process of pricking out is fiddly, but absorbing. First lever out the seedling, using a small kitchen fork or even a sturdy plant label, keeping as much root as possible. Then make a hole in the new pot or seed tray with a dibber or pencil. Gently lift the seedling, holding it by one of its leaves (never by the stem, which is very fragile at this stage), transfer it to the hole and firm it down. Water it in using a watering can with a fine rose. When filling a seed tray, use your own best judgement about spacing seedlings. Thirty per seed tray is the norm for medium-sized plants like busy lizzies. Return the pots or trays to the warm, bright windowsill and continue to keep evenly moist.

Summer bedding plants aren't frost-hardy, nor will they like a sudden transition from a warm room to the cold nights of the great outdoors. So a couple of weeks before you're ready to put them outdoors, harden them off. For the first week, place them outside for a few hours on warm, bright days, in a sheltered position, gradually increasing the amount of time they spend outdoors. In the second week, you can leave them outdoors overnight so long as no frosts are forecast.

HOW EASY?

Most bedding plants are easy to grow from seed, but some can be tricky. Here's a rough breakdown to help you make your choice.

Easy	Tricky
bellis	anagallis
bidens	begonia
brachycome	busy lizzie (impatiens)
dahlia	fuchsia
diascia	pansies and violas
felicia	petunia
forget-me-not	primula
gazania	
lobelia	**Difficult**
marigold	calceolaria
nasturtium	geranium
nemesia	(pelargonium)
nolana	mimulus
ornamental cabbage	(monkey flower)
osteospermum	solenopsis
portulaca	verbena
tobacco plant	
(nicotiana)	

GROWING FROM SEED

GROWING FROM CUTTINGS

Many of our loveliest bedding plants are actually perennials, but aren't frost hardy. Most can be overwintered indoors, but if you're stuck for space, you can keep them going (and save money) by taking cuttings – if you browse through our 'Best bedding plants' section, you'll find we have noted those that are easily propagated from cuttings.

Midsummer is generally the best time to take cuttings, with high temperatures to spur root growth, and plenty of warm weather ahead to encourage a well-established root system before winter.

First prepare several pots (a 12.5cm/5in pot will take a good number of cuttings) by filling them with cuttings compost, or with multipurpose compost mixed half and half with sharp sand from the garden centre, to provide good drainage.

To take the cuttings, select strong, young shoots and snip them off just below a leaf joint to a length of around 7.5cm/3in. Reject any spindly shoots, or any with emerging flower buds.

Trim off the lower leaves and insert the cuttings to half their length around the edge of the pot (they seem to root better here than in the middle), firming the soil down around them.

Water gently and cover the top of the pot with a polythene bag secured with an elastic band. To prevent the cuttings coming into contact with the polythene (and possibly rotting), either blow into the bag before securing it, or insert a few short canes to prop it up.

Place the pot in a warm, light (but not sunny) spot indoors. If a lot of moisture collects inside the bag, loosen it for a few hours to let it disperse.

Remove any cuttings that have obviously failed as soon as possible, to prevent the spread of rot. Once the rest of the cuttings have rooted (you'll see signs of vigorous growth, and feel a resistance if the cutting is gently tugged), transfer them to individual small pots filled with multipurpose compost. These can then be overwintered in a cool, light room and kept moderately watered. Increase the watering as the weather warms up and you'll have fine young plants just raring to go.

Tips

✔ *It's surprising how many plants will root in water, and it's a very simple way of increasing your stock. Be prepared to try anything – you've nothing to lose. Just cut off a sturdy sideshoot, trim the lower leaves and put it in a glass of water. When roots form, plant into multipurpose compost.*

✔ *If you're collecting a lot of cuttings at one time, place them in a polythene bag and seal it up to keep them as fresh as possible, until you're ready to use them.*

✔ *If a cutting threatens to flower, nip it in the bud. Flower formation takes up the energy that it should be putting into making roots.*

For a fine show of geraniums (above), take cuttings in summer (above left) and overwinter them indoors.

OVERWINTERING

Keeping perennials from year to year is well worth it, especially with more expensive plants like geraniums, marguerites and fuchsias. You need to have the room, of course – a porch or unheated conservatory is ideal, being cool, light and frost-free.

At the end of summer, listen out for frost forecasts and bring your plants in as soon as possible. It's fairly easy to dismantle a window box without causing too much root damage, but densely planted hanging baskets are a little trickier. Water beforehand, to make the roots part more easily, then tease out your chosen plants as gently as possible. Some root damage is inevitable, but growth is slowing down now and plants won't be badly harmed. Transfer your chosen plants to individual pots, making sure that the rootball is a pretty tight fit, and fill any gaps with multipurpose compost. Water to settle the compost.

You'll find that there's often a little spurt of growth at this stage, but it soon slows down as the weather gets colder. This is when you should gradually reduce watering to virtually zero, watering only when the compost is dust dry. Fuchsias and marguerites will shed their leaves in response to the colder weather and lack of watering, but geraniums will generally hang on to them, and may even flower.

When the first new shoots appear in spring, it's time to cut the plants back to promote dense and shapely new growth. The extent to which you cut back depends very much on the individual plant. A large marguerite or fuchsia can be trimmed back by a third. But if you want only a reasonable sized plant (a hanging basket fuchsia for instance), then cut all growth back to within 5cm/2in of the base. With geraniums, it's generally a matter of cutting out the woodier, less productive stems and shortening the rest by about half.

Now gradually start to increase watering, and as the plant grows, pinch out the tips of the stems to encourage an even, bushy shape. To promote extra-vigorous growth, repot plants into pots one or two sizes larger. When it's time to plant outside, harden them off in the same way as young plants raised from seed.

OVERWINTERING TUBEROUS BEGONIAS

Tuberous begonias, some of which are called 'non-stop' because of their enthusiastic flowering, are becoming increasingly popular, and ever-better varieties are introduced each year. They're so showy, and so versatile (good in sun but equally happy in shade), that it's well worth saving a few pennies by keeping the same plants going from year to year.

All you have to do is remove them from the container in autumn, before the first frosts, and clean off any soil around the base of the dish-shaped tubers. Let the foliage die back, and remove it when it's thoroughly desiccated. Store the tubers in shallow boxes, covered with a dry material such as coir or bark chips, at a minimum temperature of 10°C/50°F, in a cool room indoors.

To revive them in spring, pot them up by half-burying them in compost, concave side uppermost, leaving the top half of the tuber exposed. Keep them in a warm room, water moderately and they'll soon start to sprout. The plants aren't hardy so you'll need to grow them indoors until danger of frost has passed.

Sizzling scarlet begonias dominate this summer basket, and the tubers can be overwintered and planted afresh each year.

Top plants

There are countless numbers of plants that are suitable for hanging baskets and window boxes, but on the following pages you'll find our pick of the bunch, chosen for their good looks combined with reliability and ease of growth.

Best BEDDING PLANTS

'Bedding plants' is a handy catch-all term for a whole range of plants that give wonderful colour and form to both summer and winter baskets. They're the ones that you plant afresh each year to give your baskets and window boxes their life and impact, whether they're annual plants like lobelia or tender perennials such as geraniums and fuchsias. Some, like lamium and lysimachia, are actually completely hardy perennials, but we include them here because they're not really suitable as permanent residents – it's the younger plants that perform so well in containers.

Asteriscus

Anagallis 'Skylover'

❀ ANAGALLIS
Produces masses of five-petalled flowers, up to 2cm/¾in across, on long, arching stems all summer long. The best known form, 'Skylover', has extraordinarily intense, vivid gentian blue flowers. A newer variety, 'Sunrise' is pale orange. Plant at the edge of window boxes so that the stems can gently trail forward. Best in sun. Usually sold as seeds or plug plants by mail order suppliers. Can be propagated from cuttings and overwintered indoors.

❀ ASTERISCUS
A profusion of bright gold, daisy-like flowers from early summer to early autumn, on spreading, slightly pendulous bushes to 30cm/1ft. Thriving in full sun, it also tolerates light shade but won't produce as many flowers. A tender perennial, it can be propagated from cuttings taken in midsummer and overwintered indoors.

❀ BEGONIA
For a trouble-free display, try the semperflorens (fibrous-rooted) varieties; they're tough, reliable and remarkably easy to grow. Forming neat mounds about 15cm/6in high, they do well in sun or shade and are smothered in red, pink or white flowers from June to the first frosts. Good performers even in poor weather, they're also drought tolerant – a useful attribute in any container plant. The bronze-leaved forms are especially attractive and make an excellent foil for lighter coloured foliage plants.

❀ BELLIS (Double daisy)
A superb spring-flowering plant that has been partially eclipsed in recent years by winter-flowering pansies.

From early spring through to early summer, they produce a mass of red, pink and white, fully double daisies. Don't be tempted by the giant-flowered varieties – they lack the grace of the smaller forms. 'Pomponette' is especially lovely, producing button-like flowers just 15cm/6in high, above neat rosettes of foliage. Good in sun or shade.

❀ BIDENS

One of the very best trailing plants for hanging baskets, the filmy, fern-like foliage is studded with bright yellow flowers throughout the summer. Extremely resilient, it will happily cope with a few days of drought. Best in full sun, though surprisingly tolerant of cool, wet summers. If it has a fault, it can sometimes be a bit too vigorous, bushing out to over 60cm/2ft, so you may need to give it the occasional trim to keep it in check. A free-flowering new variety, 'Goldie' is slightly less rampant.

❀ BRACHYCOME (Swan River daisy)

A charming combination of feathery, glossy green foliage and miniature daisy-like flowers which cover the bush all summer. Growing to around 23cm/9in in a sunny spot, a range of colours is available including pale pink, white, yellow and various shades of blue. It's also one of those valuable plants that recover quickly if you forget to water it. And, rather considerately, it reminds you, because the flowers close up when watering is overdue.

❀ BUSY LIZZIE (Impatiens)

The most popular bedding plant of all, and no wonder. It is a beautiful, compact plant, growing up to 25cm/10in, and even in a poor summer will flower from June to the first frosts. Growing equally happily in sun or shade, there's an amazing range to choose from, with over 20 colours and single or double flowers (though these latter are slightly less robust in a mixed planting). Busy lizzies do wilt badly if they get too dry, but the damage isn't lasting and they rapidly perk up when watered again.

❀ CENTRADENIA

A handsome trailing plant with shiny bronze leaves. It also has small, rounded, purple flowers, but as these appear early in the season, it's best to consider it as a colourful foliage plant when planning your displays. Good in sun or partial shade, it likes to be kept moist. A tender perennial, so take cuttings in spring or midsummer and overwinter them indoors.

❀ CHRYSANTHEMUM

Of all the chrysanthemum varieties, the compact and bushy Yoder chrysanthemums are the very best for creating a spectacular splash of colour in early autumn displays, though they will only last for a few weeks. Buy small plants just coming into flower and treat them as instant colour. In their second and third years they grow rather too big for hanging baskets and window boxes, so when they've finished their dazzling display, move them to a

Convolvulus sabatius

sunny, sheltered, well-drained spot in the garden where they should grow happily for years to come.

❀ CINERARIA (Senecio)

One of the finest silver foliage plants, providing a very effective contrast with flowering plants. The feathery-leaved 'Silver Dust' is the most compact at just 23cm/9in. Like most silver-leaved plants it performs best in full sun, and is extremely tolerant of drought, which is why it's useful for hanging baskets. It's a slightly tender perennial but becomes ungainly in its second season, so is best treated as an annual.

❀ CONVOLVULUS

The perennial *Convolvulus sabatius* has very pretty, trumpet-shaped, blue/purple flowers and shiny green foliage. This really is an excellent trailing plant for sunny positions, cascading as much as 37.5cm/15in during the season, and while it's highly attractive in its own right, it also makes a superb foil for other plants. Copes well with the occasional dry spell, recovering quickly when watered. Take cuttings in summer and overwinter indoors.

✿ CORDYLINE

Bought as small plants, around 20cm/8in high, these palm-like shrubs produce a fountain of narrow leaves, and make an eye-catching focal point for baskets and boxes. However, they need to be used with care – they provide a slightly exotic touch and can look out of place in traditional plantings. A number of variegated forms are available, from cream to plum-purple. They aren't hardy, so overwinter them indoors. As they get bigger, move them into large pots to make the most of them.

✿ DIASCIA

The spikes of small, shell-like flowers are produced throughout summer on mat-forming plants to a height of 20cm/8in. Surprisingly drought tolerant. A lovely thing, but use it with discretion – its subtle beauty is somewhat lost if viewed from a distance, so place it in hanging baskets or window boxes that will be admired in close-up. New shades are being introduced every year, ranging through apricot and pink to coral and lilac. Slightly tender so take cuttings as a precaution against winter losses.

Diascia

Gazania

✿ FELICIA

An attractive, bushy plant up to 30cm/1ft high, producing a host of small, daisy flowers (blue with a gold centre), throughout summer. The green-leaved forms are the most readily available, but there's a very striking green and cream variety that's worth tracking down. Felicia prefers to be kept moist but can shrug off the occasional drought. Needs sun to perform well. A tender perennial, so be sure to take cuttings and overwinter them indoors.

✿ FUCHSIA

For sheer, breathtaking showmanship, fuchsias are unbeatable. The gorgeous, dancing flowers, either in single or even more exuberant double forms, provide a spectacular display of colour from summer to the first frosts. But they do need a little cosseting. Their most important requirement is moist soil; if it dries out the flowers and buds will usually fall off, and it can take six weeks for the plant to fully recover. So it's essential to water them regularly, especially if they're in a

hot sunny position. Many gardeners prefer to grow them in light shade, where they'll be just as happy and will need less watering. For best results, pinch out the growing tips when planting out to encourage strong, dense growth.

Bush fuchsias make dramatic centrepieces for hanging baskets and window boxes. There really are some glorious varieties available, and in a wide range of colour combinations. Our favourites include 'Annabel', with very large blooms of white tinted with pale pink, and 'Thalia', with clusters of long, slim, orange-red, tubular flowers that make a lovely contrast with the deep green, red-backed foliage.

As for the trailing forms, use them to cascade down the sides of your containers. Again, the range is terrific, and one of the most reliable old favourites is 'Cascade', with a pale pink body and deep carmine skirt. For maximum impact though, look out for the new 'California Dreamers' varieties with their enormous double flowers up to 10cm/4in across.

The majority of bedding fuchsias are tender perennials, so if you want to keep them for next year, you'll have to overwinter them indoors in a frost-free spot. Cuttings can be taken at almost any time, but are most successful in midsummer.

✿ GAZANIA

Large, showy, daisy flowers in a range of colour mixes from deep orange to pale yellow. They're produced throughout summer on

BEST BEDDING PLANTS

spreading bushes to a height of 30cm/1ft. Some also have attractive silver or variegated foliage. However, you'll need to position them with care – many varieties open only if they're in a sunny spot, and, since the flowers face upwards, you need a low-level basket or box to enjoy them fully. Take cuttings in summer and overwinter indoors.

❀ GERANIUM (Pelargonium)

For maximum colour with minimum effort, grow geraniums, the undisputed stars of the summer display. They really are remarkable plants, flowering their hearts out all summer long, and unlike fuchsias, which can be quite demanding, they'll survive incredible amounts of neglect. They can happily cope with being dried out for several days, bouncing back to glowing health when you do finally water them. There's a variety to suit everyone, in bush and trailing forms.

The bush varieties, with large globes of flower and rounded, slightly scalloped leaves, are perfect as a centrepiece for hanging baskets and window boxes. Those with double or semi-double flowers are the showiest, but tend to catch and hold rain (or a badly aimed squirt from the hosepipe) and can rot.

The singles have fewer petals, but compensate with more flower spikes, so are just as colourful and completely rain-proof. There are so many fine varieties, in colours to suit any planting scheme, that it's difficult to pick favourites, but we're especially fond of deep cherry red 'Doris Moore' and blush-pink 'Highfield's Appleblossom'.

To cascade down the side of hanging baskets or window boxes, the trailing or ivy-leaved forms are unbeatable for troublefree colour and impact. Two of the best are 'Rouletta' (also known as 'Mexicana'), the white petals edged with cerise, and 'L'Elégante', with pale pink flowers and white-edged leaves that rather prettily turn pink in times of drought. The other great group of trailers are the geraniums variously known as 'Swiss', 'balcon' or 'continental'. They give superb displays, trailing as much as 90cm/3ft and sending out hundreds of sprays of airy flowers. The most compact form is the recently introduced 'Evka', whose cream-edged foliage makes a striking contrast with the bright salmon flowers.

All geraniums do best in full sun, and are tender perennials, so bring them indoors to overwinter before the first frosts. Like fuchsias, it's also very easy to take cuttings and it's a great way to increase your stock of these lovely plants.

Helichrysum 'Variegatum'

❀ GLECHOMA (Nepeta)

A fast-growing, trailing plant with handsome, kidney-shaped leaves, variegated green and white. Deservedly popular, it's good in sun or shade and provides an attractive background for other plants. But try to keep it evenly moist – if it dries out it can die back and look scruffy. Revive glechoma by trimming back hard, but it can take some weeks to recover fully.

❀ HELICHRYSUM

One of the very finest foliage plants, adding structure and colour to any planting scheme. A spreading trailer, the leaves are rounded with a velvety texture. Of the two silver forms, the larger-leaved variety is particularly vigorous but is easily trimmed back if it's taking over, while its pretty small-leaved cousin is much more restrained. Both thrive in sun, as does the lovely gold-flecked grey form. The luscious 'Limelight', with gorgeous lime-green foliage, is best in partial shade. All are virtually indestructible.

Geranium 'Century Scarlet'

Lobelia 'Riviera Blue Splash'

❀ LAMIUM

An increasingly popular and colourful foliage plant, equally good in summer and, if kept in sheltered positions, in winter baskets. Two of the best are 'White Nancy', a compact trailer with glowing green-edged silver foliage, and 'Gold Nuggets', which is bright gold with a white flash. Look out, too, for the new, silver 'Hermann's Pride'. Reasonably drought tolerant, and happy in sun or shade. At the end of the season, move them to your border – they make excellent ground cover plants.

❀ LOBELIA

A stalwart of summer displays, with a haze of flowers from early summer to mid autumn, happy in sun or partial shade. For the best results, keep it moist – it hates to dry out. It's not so difficult to revive early in the season if you water it and cut it back a little to stimulate fresh new growth, but if you let it dry out in midsummer, the chances are that it will die back completely. The best of the bush forms are the 'Riviera'

series, especially 'Blue Splash', which is a gorgeous rippled mix of white and blue. Try underplanting a moss basket just with bush lobelia – when it's fully grown the effect is wonderful. For trailing varieties, choose the free-flowering 'Regatta' series – they've got a 'Blue Splash' too. The double-flowered, blue 'Kathleen Mallard' is the prettiest of all, but flowers late in the season,

and not quite as prolifically. In most schemes, white or blue lobelias are the most effective – the reds and pinks can look insipid.

❀ LOTUS

A beautiful, silver-filigree, sun-loving plant which cascades as much as 90cm/3ft in a season. In a hot summer it may produce its remarkable red, claw-like flowers. It can tolerate drought for short periods but will suffer if badly neglected. A tender perennial, it can be overwintered indoors. Take cuttings from sideshoots from early- to midsummer.

❀ LYSIMACHIA

Happy in sun or shade, this is a lovely trailing plant with neat, heart-shaped leaves that are studded with buttercup flowers from midsummer to early autumn. Available in green, yellow and variegated forms, of which the green and gold 'Outback Sunset' is outstanding. They need regular watering – if they dry out, they have a tendency to collapse, often taking weeks to recover.

Filigree lotus displaying its remarkable red flowers.

Marguerite 'Peach Cheeks'

❀ MARGUERITE (Argyranthemum)

One of the very best plants for sunny spots, forming a neat dome of large daisy flowers in a range of colours from white through pink, to peach and gold. The feathery foliage is bright, fresh green, though there are also some very pretty silver-leaved forms like 'Royal Haze'. The most vigorous varieties, growing to around 60cm/2ft, would look top-heavy in a hanging basket, but are excellent for larger window boxes. For a more compact habit, look out for double white 'Snowflake', clear pink 'Summer Pink' and soft creamy yellow 'Lemon Delight'. Marguerites are tender perennials, so overwinter them indoors in a light frost-free place. Cuttings are best taken in late summer.

❀ MARIGOLD

You either love them or hate them, but either way there's no disputing the stunning impact of the bright orange or yellow flowers. The only white variety, 'French Vanilla', is lovely but may grow too tall for a small basket, so pick the smaller, more compact forms of French marigold such as double-flowered 'Orange Boy' and 'Yellow Boy', both reaching a diminutive 15cm/6in. All varieties thrive in sun, flower prolifically from an early stage, and cope well with occasional lapses in watering.

❀ MIMULUS (Monkey flower)

These are colourful, nasturtium-like flowers, useful for shade, but it is essential they are kept moist. 'Malibu Orange' forms a neat bush just 15cm/6in high, with masses of small, vivid orange flowers all summer, while 'Pastel Magic Mixed', growing to 25cm/10in, is a splendid selection of velvet-textured flowers in shades of yellow, cream and pink. If you let them dry out, you should cut them

French marigold 'Safari Primrose'

Nasturtium 'Primrose Jewel'

which are grown from cuttings , including the orange, trailing 'Hermine Grasshof'.

❀ NEMESIA

The annual forms, although very pretty, are not ideal for hanging baskets and window boxes because they usually finish flowering by midsummer, but the recently introduced perennial varieties are well worth growing. Similar in many ways to diascia, with small flowers freely produced all summer. They are very charming in close-up, especially as they're also heavily scented. Try 'Innocence', which is pure white with a yellow eye, or rose pink 'Melanie'. All prefer a moist soil, in sun. You can overwinter the perennial varieties indoors or take cuttings.

back hard and then water and feed, to encourage fresh growth and a new flush of flowers.

❀ NASTURTIUM

With their spectacular, trumpet-like flowers in the most vivid yellows, oranges and scarlets, these vigorous plants can overpower any display unless used with discretion. The 'Whirlybird' varieties are the best choice because the leaves are neater than most and the flowers are well displayed above them. Pop four or five seeds in when planting up a basket and thin out to three plants as they grow. Alternatively, try one of the very pretty double varieties

❀ NICOTIANA (Tobacco plant)

Most varieties grow too tall and bushy for hanging baskets, but would make a striking addition to larger window boxes. They are remarkably easy to grow, flower for months on end (whatever the

Nemesia 'KLM'·

Nicotiana 'Havana Lime Green'

Nolana 'Blue Bird'

✤ ORNAMENTAL CABBAGE

Few plants arouse as much passion. Either (like us) you love them, or you hate them, but nothing quite matches these extraordinary brassicas for their spectacular displays. Bred from the edible varieties, they produce open, frilly heads in a glorious range of white, cream, rose and purple. The 'Northern Lights' series is especially colourful and can grow to 45cm/18in across. Dramatic, instant colour for autumn and winter, but by spring they'll be past their best and will need replacing with something far less controversial and far less fun.

✤ OSTEOSPERMUM

These lovely South African daisies are much too tall for hanging baskets, but look wonderful in large window boxes. Most grow to weather), tolerate drought, and are happy in sun or partial shade. The new 'Merlin' series grows to just 20cm/8in, the 'Domino' series to 30cm/1ft. Both are available in a wide range of colours ('Domino Salmon Pink' is especially good), but sadly, neither is scented.

✤ NOLANA

A lovely, low-growing semi-trailer that produces masses of large, trumpet-like flowers throughout the summer. Especially tolerant of hot, dry conditions, which makes it an ideal candidate for baskets, despite its rather annoying habit of keeping its flowers closed on dull, chilly days. 'Blue Bird' is a gorgeous sky blue with a distinct creamy-white centre. You will probably have to grow from seed, since young plants aren't readily available.

Ornamental cabbages

45cm/18in or more, but there are more compact forms like 'Glistening White' and 'Salmon Queen', both reaching 30cm/1ft. All are drought tolerant but need as much sun as possible, since the flowers tend to close in dull conditions. Most varieties are tender perennials, and plants (or cuttings) can be overwintered indoors.

❀ PANSY & VIOLA

Although they're on sale throughout the year, pansies are at their best in winter and spring. They rarely do as well in summer – heat makes them straggly, and they very quickly succumb to drought. 'Universal' and 'Ultima' pansies have been specially bred to cope with the cold of winter. Compact and bushy (just 20cm/8in high), they start flowering in autumn, carry on through any mild spells in winter, and burst into a magnificent show of colour from the first warm days of spring right through to May. 'Ultima' hybrids have the slight edge because of the fantastic colour range available.

Petunia 'Frenzy Chiffon'

Violas have much daintier and more numerous flowers, and great charm. They're particularly effective in boxes or baskets that are viewed in close-up, since the flowers make little impact from a distance. In the past they've only really been considered as good spring-flowering plants, but the breeders have come up trumps with 'Sorbet' violas. They are available in some lovely colours, are weather resistant, and will flower as long as winter pansies. They're also beautifully neat, reaching just 12.5cm/5in. Like pansies, they can be grown in sun or partial shade, and should be kept watered through any long dry spells.

❀ PETUNIA

Excellent sun-loving flowers for summer displays, and available in a wide variety of forms. The traditional bush petunias grow to 30cm/1ft or so, and the best of these are the multiflora types which are

Winter pansy 'Universal Plus'

Plectranthus

Primula 'Wanda Supreme'

more tolerant of poor weather than the slightly larger grandifloras. But do, we beg of you, pick the single-flowered forms. The doubles are incredibly tempting, but they collapse like a damp dishcloth as soon as it rains.

The new 'Fantasy' and 'Junior' petunias are extremely compact, growing to just 20cm/8in, and look superb in both baskets and boxes. The flowers are produced in abundance throughout summer – they smother the foliage and the overall effect is of a delightful mound of colour. But they do insist on a weekly feed to do well.

'Million Bells' is another choice new form, producing masses of small, bell-like flowers on low mounds of neat, semi-cascading foliage which spills over the edges of baskets and boxes. Only violet and pink are available at the moment, though no doubt more colours will be introduced.

But if it's maximum impact you want, grow the great, surging 'Surfinia' and 'Wave' types, bushing out to an immense size, with the ability to trail to 1.2m/4ft. One or

two plants will swamp a basket, flowering continuously from midsummer to autumn. In lots of lovely colours, they're rain resistant and very drought tolerant. For sheer size and flower power, they take some beating.

❀ PLECTRANTHUS

A vigorous trailing plant, excellent for summer displays, with oval, scalloped leaves edged in white. Good in sun or partial shade, cascading as much as 90cm/3ft. Extremely drought tolerant, and a superb foil for more colourful flowering plants. A tender perennial, it is easily propagated from cuttings taken in summer and overwintered indoors.

❀ POLYANTHUS & PRIMULA

The showiest members of the primrose family are polyanthus, with flowers held in clusters atop sturdy stems. The best strain is 'Crescendo', growing to 30cm/1ft. It's completely winter hardy, producing its first flowers extra early (from midwinter onwards), and there's a terrific range of jewel-

like colours available. For reliably hardy primulas, forming low rosettes of leaves and flowers, choose the 'Wanda' varieties which are just as colourful and flower from early spring onwards. All grow equally well in sun or partial shade.

❀ POLYGONUM

Polygonum capitatum is a most attractive, mat-forming semi-trailer, to a diminutive 10cm/4in or so. The dark green leaves are marked with handsome, deep red chevrons, and globes massed with tiny flowers are produced from early summer to the first frosts. 'Pink Bubbles' is particularly attractive. A tough, resilient plant, happy in sun or shade.

❀ PORTULACA

With its needle-like succulent leaves and brilliant colours, this is a good plant for a sun-drenched position, with saucer-shaped single and double flowers on a 15cm/6in semi-trailing plant. You're most likely to be growing it from seed, so look out for the newer strains like 'Sundial' that don't close up in disgust when

Scaevola

Verbena 'Peaches and Cream'

Solenopsis

the sun goes in. Exceedingly drought tolerant, it really relishes a hot summer.

❀ SCAEVOLA
Few trailing plants are as good as this. It doesn't really cascade, rather it spreads, to as much as 45cm/18in, producing hundreds of blue flowers that are rather like large lobelias. 'Blue Fan' and the more compact 'New Wonder' are the best forms, needing sun and a moist soil for the most spectacular display. A tender perennial, it can be overwintered in a frost-free place, and cuttings can be taken in spring or midsummer.

❀ SOLENOPSIS (Isotoma/Laurentia)
Forming a mound of feathery green foliage to 23cm/9in, covered in small, shooting star flowers, all summer. 'Blue Star' is lovely, with its lightly fragrant, sky blue flowers. Pink and white flowered forms are available too, but the latter, in particular, hasn't the same impact as the blue. It can be grown from seed, but young plants are widely available. Take cuttings in summer and overwinter like geraniums.

❀ SUTURA (Bacopa)
A small leaved and extremely neat trailing plant, ideal for a sunny position, cascading as much as 45cm/18in and covered in masses of tiny flowers throughout summer. Pure white 'Snowflake' is the most readily available, but lilac-pink forms are being introduced, some of which have a more bushy, upright growth habit. Cuttings can be taken in early spring or late summer and overwintered indoors.

❀ VERBENA
Gloriously colourful, sun-loving plants, admired by all. The bush forms are excellent but the new trailing varieties are even more desirable. The 'Tapien' series, in shades of blue, purple and pink, produces clusters of pin-cushion flowers in such abundance that they completely hide the foliage. More compact and less straggly than some of the older trailing verbenas, they are also more weather resistant and will flower throughout the summer. A sister series, 'Temari', has recently been introduced, with larger leaves and flowers in pink or scarlet. 'Pink Parfait' is more of a semi-trailer, with extra-large fragrant flowers in two shades of pink – quite delightful. All are tender perennials which can be overwintered in a frost-free position indoors or from cuttings taken in mid to late summer.

Best BULBS

Chionodoxa

Spring bulbs are essential additions when you're planting up hanging baskets and window boxes in autumn for winter displays. They simmer away under the surface, bursting into glorious colour and flower as the days lengthen and the weather warms. And don't forget the summer bulbs (some of which are actually corms or tubers, but who's counting?). The neater varieties of dahlia are lovely for window boxes, and tuberous begonias put on a wonderful display in any container.

❀ BEGONIA

The tuberous begonias are tremendously showy plants for all summer containers, with an electric range of colours that shine out in sun and even more brightly in shade. Great mixers, but also good *en masse* in a basket. We're great fans of the pendulous varieties, the heavy double flowers (and a scattering of singles) which dangle most lusciously. Look out for the new 'Champagne', which promises to be especially free-flowering. For maximum flower production, keep evenly moist. They are grown from dish-shaped tubers (see page 77) which can be dried off in autumn, stored over winter and started into growth again the following spring.

❀ CHIONODOXA

Also known as 'glory of the snow', chionodoxa is a neat petite plant growing to no more than 10cm/4in, with white-centred blue flowers like little stars. Useful for early interest in boxes and baskets, flowering in early spring – plant in generous clumps for maximum impact. White and pink forms also available. Sun or partial shade.

The pendulous form of tuberous begonia, planted en masse *in a window box.*

Crocus 'Zwanenburg Bronze'

❀ CROCUS

Another treat for early in the year. Earliest of all are the dainty specie crocus, making their appearance in late winter, and though they're small (7.5cm/3in), they can be extremely colourful – take rich, deep violet 'Ruby Giant', for instance, or glowing gold 'EP Bowles'. For early spring colour, there are the fat Dutch crocus, a little taller and slightly less elegant, but single-colour groups can be charming. Grow in sun, where they open up into wide stars.

❀ DAFFODIL (Narcissus)

Daffodils are a sheer delight, the one indispensable spring bulb, and should be used with abandon in both hanging baskets and window boxes, in sun and shade. Their image is 'bold and gold', but this is a family of plants with more cards up their sleeves than there are in a whole pack, and there's an astonishing range of colour and form.

In hanging baskets, where anything tall and large-flowered will look totally out of proportion, exploit the wide range of miniatures. One of the smallest, at 12.5cm/5in, is the exquisite, gold *Narcissus cyclamineus*, the petals curved right back so that the flowers resemble half of a very

narrow Christmas cracker. Just a little taller is *N. canaliculatus*, with yellow-cupped, white-petalled flowers held three or four to a stem, and sweetly scented. Then there's the perennial favourite, 'Tête-à-Tête', a 15cm/6in marvel with its multiple heads of golden flowers, and its sister 'Quince', at 20cm/8in, in soft primrose. And 'Jack Snipe', 'Sundisc', 'Minnow', 'Little Witch', 'Jumblie', 'Golden Bells'... we

could go on and on, because there are dozens of these little wonders.

They can all, of course, take their place equally happily in window boxes, but if the box is in a sheltered spot, you can afford to go for some of the taller varieties in the 30-35cm/12-14in range. Beauties like early-flowering 'February Gold' and lemon-cupped, white-petalled 'February Silver'. Or early spring flowering, multi-headed 'Thalia', whose milky-white scented flowers have a breathtaking grace. You might also want to try some of the showier daffodils which look more at home in a container than in the open garden. Ruffled doubles like white 'Acropolis', or the extraordinary 'split corona' types, where the trumpet is split and flattened back against the petals. There are some lovely colours here, especially in the peach/apricot range.

Narcissus 'February Gold'

❀ DAHLIA

We confess to once having been a bit reticent about dahlias – the stiff formality of the exhibition types put us off. But there are some charming dwarf varieties flowering from July to the first frosts. The singles are the most appealing, and mix well with other flowers. 'Bambino', for instance, forms a neat 25cm/10in dome of white blooms with a prominent yellow centre – lovely in a window box devoted to cool yellows and whites. The tubers can be overwintered in the same way as begonias (see page 77).

❀ HYACINTH

Far too top-heavy for hanging baskets but useful for early colour in window boxes, especially if you occasionally open the window to drink in the marvellous scent. And do try some of the more unusual colours, rather than sticking to pink, white and blue. 'Distinction' is a wonderful mix of beetroot and

Scilla mischtschenkoana

purple, 'Woodstock' a rich magenta. For a lighter, less formal effect, try the 'Roman' hyacinths, multi-stemmed with looser, more airy heads of flower. All hyacinths are equally good in sun or partial shade.

❀ IPHEION

Not nearly as widely grown as they deserve, these are lovely star-shaped flowers for early spring. For a clear white, choose 15cm/6in 'Album', for a blue, the slightly shorter 'Wisley Blue' or extra-early azure blue 'Rolf Fiedler' which is best in a sheltered position. Grow in sun or partial shade.

❀ IRIS RETICULATA

Delightful late winter flowers for window boxes, where you can stand indoors and gaze down on their exquisite colours and patternings. 'Cantab', for instance, the pale blue of a spring sky with white flecks and a tongue of yellow on the lower petals. Or the warm red-purple of 'JS Dijt', which is especially vigorous, and scented. None grow to more than 15cm/6in, and all are best in sun.

❀ MUSCARI

Most gardeners are familiar with the little grape hyacinth, *Muscari armenaiacum*, with its spikes of blue bobbles, but there are some slightly more unusual varieties that are worth looking out for. Violet-blue *M. comosum* 'Plumosum', for instance, which sends up feathery plumes of flower to 15cm/6in or more in May. And, even lovelier, early spring flowering *M. latifolium*, which looks like a miniature red-hot poker, changing colour from blue-purple at the bottom to sky blue at the top. Best in sun.

❀ SCILLA

The most familiar of the scillas is little *Scilla siberica*, with its early spring flowers of brilliant blue dangling on wiry 15cm/6in stems – lovely in generous clumps in both baskets and boxes. There's a white form too, which is equally good. Another scilla worth tracking down is *S. mischtschenkoana* (awful name, sometimes sold under the equally tongue-twisting *S. tubergeniana*). It's a particularly fresh shade of palest blue, looking

Muscari

Snowdrops with dwarf narcissi.

Tulipa praestans 'Unicum'

almost silvery from a distance and, at just 10cm/4in, a very dainty thing. Remarkably early flowering too – in milder districts it can make its appearance in late winter. All are good in sun or partial shade.

❀ SNOWDROP (Galanthus)

It's impossible to get through late winter without a few snowdrops about the place, and they're superb little plants for boxes and baskets, especially in shadier positions. There are singles aplenty, but it's the doubles that make most impact in a winter display. Grow them in fat clumps so that you have a few to spare for picking for the house. And if you can, buy them 'in the green' in spring. These plants, which have been lifted after flowering, establish much more readily than dried bulbs, and they're often advertised in the small ads of gardening magazines. Then all you have to do is pot them up, sink them in a shady spot in the garden through summer, and transfer them to their basket or box when planting up your winter schemes.

❀ TULIP

Along with daffodils, these are the stars of spring displays, available in an endless variety of colours, shapes and sizes. Tricky for hanging baskets though, since most of the shorter varieties have the typical fat tulip leaves which would cover an undue amount of basket. But there are just a few varieties with less aggressive foliage. Two species of tulips, for example – 20cm/8in *Tulipa turkestanica* (ivory-yellow with a gold centre) for early spring, and the slightly shorter *Tulipa tarda* (starry gold petals tipped with cream) for mid spring. Even more richly coloured are the pulchella hybrids – tiny things at only 12.5cm/5in, in a range of violet, purple and magenta, flowering extra-early in late winter or early spring.

There's a much wider choice of tulips for window boxes, starting with the invaluable Kaufmanniana and Greigii hybrids, so often recognisable by the attractive maroon striping to the leaves. The average height is only 20cm/8in, so they're ideal for boxes, and a bright bunch they are too. Kaufmannianas

generally appear in early spring, in a huge range of colours – we particularly like 'Heart's Delight', an uplifting carmine edged in palest rose. The Greigiis are in flower a month or so later, and 'Cape Cod' is a tried and tested favourite – warm apricot edged with yellow, and bronze yellow within. *Tulipa praestans* 'Unicum' is another early delight with its cream-edged leaves.

The double-flowered early varieties are well worth investigating too, growing to around 25cm/10in and flowering in April. 'Peach Blossom' is a ruffled romance of rose pink tones, 'Willemsoord' a peony-like carmine flower, the petal edges lightly feathered in white. And taller varieties of tulip are well worth considering in a sheltered spot, opening up all sorts of possibilities from the riotously feathered 'parrot' tulips to the sleek serenity of lily-flowered varieties.

Always place tulips in a sunny position because the inside of the flowers can be astonishingly beautiful, and the sun will encourage them to open up.

Best PERENNIALS

These are the plants that save you time and money, because they live in the window box or hanging basket all year round. Some, like box and conifers, are simple foils for more glamorous flowering plants, but others are much more showy. A pieris, for instance, with its spring display of bright red new leaves and dangling clusters of white flower, packs quite a punch.

❀ AJUGA

Good edging plants, mainly used for winter displays, the low rosettes of variegated foliage giving a splash of colour in sun or shade. 'Burgundy Glow' is a lovely blend of bronze, pink and white, and even more striking is 'Rainbow' (sometimes sold as 'Multicolor') which is a hectic mix of dark green, creamy yellow, red and bronze. At the end of the season, replant in the garden – they make excellent ground cover.

❀ ALPINES

Many alpines love a hot, dry spot, making them perfect for a long-lasting, easy-care basket or box. Low growing, mat-forming sedums and sempervivums for instance, which make a pretty tapestry in a wire basket, with good contrasts of evergreen leaf shape and colour, and pretty summer flowers. Campanulas are useful too, especially the vigorous *Campanula portenschlagiana* which can be given a box or basket to itself, swamping it with trailing sprays of lavender blue stars from early summer to late autumn.

❀ AUCUBA (Laurel)

Young plants of the spotted laurels, with large, glossy leaves heavily mottled or splashed with gold, look great in winter window boxes, especially when teamed up with gold flowers – golden pansies, say, followed by primroses and narcissi in spring. Easy-going plants, they can be transferred to the garden to grow, where they can be used to light up a shady corner.

Aucuba (*Laurel*)

❀ BAY (Laurus)

'Kitchen' bays (unshaped plants, usually found in the herb section at the garden centre), are another useful evergreen for winter boxes. The rich, deep green of the foliage mixes well with other colours, and the occasional leaf snippings add flavour to winter casseroles. It is, however, slightly tender, so cover with horticultural fleece or sacking if severe frosts are forecast. Best in full sun in a sheltered position.

❀ BOX (Buxus)

With its dense cover of small evergreen leaves, box is ideal for clipping into puddings, globes or fancier shapes like spirals. Especially good in a formal window box scheme, either as a centrepiece

Ajuga 'Purpurea' with asters and heathers.

or as an interesting 'full stop' at either end. Very slow-growing, box is a good permanent ingredient for a low maintenance window box where only a few bedding plants are needed for seasonal colour. Good in sun or partial shade.

❀ CONIFERS
Like box, conifers are excellent plants for both hanging baskets and window boxes, and they come in some wonderful shapes and colours. *Juniperus squamata* 'Blue Star' makes a low bush, covered in spiky needles of steely blue. For a dome to top a hanging basket, try bright gold *Chamaecyparis lawsoniana* 'Aurea Densa'. Then there are all the greens to be explored, from the very deepest, to fresh, bright, apple green. The dwarf varieties (look for 'nana', 'pygmaea', 'minima' etc. in their names) are incredibly slow growing and will last for years. Most conifers colour-up best in sun.

❀ COTONEASTER MICROPHYLLUS
A profusion of tiny, deep green leaves on a low, spreading plant, with the bonus of spring flowers, followed by red berries in autumn. Wonderful as the centrepiece in a winter basket, but equally useful in boxes. If it spreads a little too far over time, just trim back some of the more vigorous stems. Equally good in sun and partial shade.

❀ EUONYMUS
Among the many evergreen varieties of euonymus are some invaluable little plants for window boxes and hanging baskets. Many forms of *Euonymus fortunei* are naturally dwarf, and 'Emerald 'n' Gold' is one of the best loved for the generous

margin of gold on each leaf that looks especially cheery in winter. There are also some very attractive varieties of *Euonymus japonicus*, but they're only reliably hardy in milder districts. Very shade tolerant.

❀ FERNS
Tremendously architectural plants and lovely for shady positions. If they're evergreen, that's even better news, because they'll look good through winter too. For a delicate tracery of fronds, look out for the soft shield fern *Polystichum setiferum*. For undivided, lance-shaped fronds, try glossy, bright green *Asplenium scolopendrium*, which has some interesting frilly-edged variants.

❀ GAULTHERIA
Also known as the partridge berry, *Gaultheria procumbens* makes a neat, low mound of dark green leaves which take on bronze tints in winter. Add to this the bright red berries and you've a very pretty picture for a winter basket. They prefer a shady position, plenty of moisture and must be grown in ericaceous (lime-free) compost.

❀ HEATHERS
Heathers make good summer container plants but it's in winter, when anything that flowers is at a premium, that they really come into their own. The froth of small flowers looks very effective against the solidity of conifers or the large leaves of evergreens such as skimmia. The two best varieties for winter and spring flower are *Erica carnea* and *Erica* x *darleyensis*, in a wide range of whites, pinks and purples. Like all heathers they need full sun, but they don't insist on a lime-free soil, so any multipurpose compost will suit. For foliage colour, track down varieties like *Calluna vulgaris* 'Robert Chapman' which is gold in summer, orange-red in winter, and prefers an ericaceous compost. Showy *Erica gracilis* with its rose-purple flowers is a good plant for autumn colour in a sheltered spot, but won't last much beyond Christmas.

❀ HEBE
It's the foliage hebes that are so useful in winter schemes. We'd recommend small-leaved, totally hardy plants like the blue-grey

Hebe pimeleoides *'Quicksilver'*

cushions of 'Pagei' or the bright green domes of 'Emerald Green'. Then there's the hebe that thinks it's a conifer; *Hebe cupressoides*, looking for all the world like a miniature cypress; grey-green 'Boughton Dome' is the most widely available. But one winter hebe to be wary of is the larger-leaved *Hebe* x *franciscana*, usually offered as a cream/green variegated plant with blue-purple flowers. It's fine in milder, coastal districts but not reliably hardy inland. Grow hebes in the brightest possible position.

✿ IVY (Hedera)

Indispensable ivy – as useful in summer as in winter. The smaller-leaved forms are the least rampant, and there are some lovely colour variations from basic green, through yellow, gold, silver and cream variegations. The cheapest way of buying them is in the bedding plant section (although it is a perennial) at the garden centre and while these 'bedding' ivies are rarely named, you should find an excellent selection. Gold-variegated varieties are best in sun, the rest in anything from full sun to heavy shade.

✿ HEUCHERA

The coloured-leaf forms of heuchera are excellent in winter baskets and boxes, especially in a shady spot. 'Palace Purple' is one of our favourites, forming a mound of large, maple-like leaves in deep, dramatic bronze-purple – lovely planted with plum-toned pansies or pink heathers. Or you could add a touch of frost with 'Pewter Moon', which is silver-marbled. They are valuable garden plants, too, so don't throw them away when dismantling winter displays.

✿ HOSTA

One of the most fashionable of all garden plants, hostas can also be grown in hanging baskets and window boxes. Forming elegant rosettes of sculpted leaves, they're invaluable for a shady position. Use young plants of the smaller varieties like white-edged 'Ground Master' and green and gold 'Gold Edger' – they look an absolute picture when mixed with ferns. They both relish the same moist conditions.

✿ LONICERA NITIDA

This tiny-leaved, evergreen member of the honeysuckle family looks lovely clipped and is especially useful for formal boxes. It does, however, have ambitions to be quite a large plant, so will probably outgrow its allotted space in two or three seasons. In addition to the mid-green form, there's greeny-gold

Ivy (Hedera)

Hosta fortunei *var.* aureomarginata

Acid-loving Pieris formosa

'Baggesen's Gold' (best in sun), and silver and green 'Silver Beauty'.

❀ PERNETTYA

Pernettyas are valued for their plump berries which last right through winter. Produced in clusters against tiny, dark green leaves, they range in colour from white, through pink, to cherry red. Great in a simple winter box planted with pansies in a toning colour. Best in sun and must have a lime-free (ericaceous) compost.

❀ PIERIS (Forest flame)

Dramatic evergreens with cascades of narrow leaves, flame red when young, and long dangling clusters of white flower in spring. The white-variegated forms are lovely, but don't produce as many flowers. Especially good for winter window boxes in sun or partial shade, but they must have a lime-free compost. They will eventually grow quite large, but can be transferred to the garden to grow on if the soil is peaty.

❀ SANTOLINA (Cotton lavender)

Best in window boxes rather than hanging baskets, *Santolina chamaecyparissus* is a neatly domed, silver-grey shrub covered in finely-dissected leaves on white-felted stems. Lemon yellow flowers, like small buttons, are produced in midsummer. Dwarf forms are available which grow to a maximum of 30cm/1ft. Keep them looking their best by clipping them back after flowering. Must have full sun.

❀ SKIMMIA

These are classics for winter colour, with a compact cover of glossy, dark green leaves and clusters of brilliant red berries – very Christmassy, and a lovely background plant for a window box in sun or partial shade. But if you want berries again next year, you need to buy both a male and female plant so that they cross-pollinate, or the hermaphrodite *Skimmia reevesiana*. For pretty pink clusters of winter flower buds (but no berries), opt for the glossy, dark-leaved *Skimmia japonica* 'Rubella'.

Best EDIBLES

HERBS

If you're short on garden space (or have no garden at all), it's good to grow a few edible plants in your hanging baskets and window boxes. Herbs are undoubtedly the easiest of all, but fruit and vegetables are well worth the extra care and attention, just to get that unbeatable home-grown, fresh-picked flavour.

HERBS

❀ BASIL

A delicious herb, but a fussy one. It hates to be cold, so don't plant it out until early summer when the weather is reliably mild. In addition to the plain green forms, look out for the frilly 'lettuce leaf' types and the extraordinary 'Purple Ruffles', which is an unearthly pearl-purple. If you track down a herb specialist, you'll find varieties with added flavour – the typical basil taste plus anything from lemon to aniseed or cinnamon. Keep well watered (but not soggy) in dry weather, and pinch off any

Sweet marjoram

flowers to promote leaf growth. An annual, so plant afresh each year. Must have full sun.

❀ CHIVES

Neat clumps of bright green, reed-like leaves, very easy to grow, and good in any window box in sun or partial shade. They can even be used in ornamental schemes, where the lilac pompon flowers are highly decorative and, like the leaves, mildly onion flavoured – very pretty and tasty in a mixed salad. A perennial, but dies back in winter. Keep well watered in hot weather.

❀ FENNEL

You might think that fennel is too tall for a window box because in the garden it can grow to 1.5m/5ft or more, but the foliage is so filmy and feathery that it's never too imposing, and it's easy enough to cut it back now and again. The bronze-leaved form is especially striking. Grow in sun. Delicious in fish and cheese dishes, and best grown afresh from seed each year.

❀ MARJORAM

One of the most useful (and attractive) marjorams for sunny boxes and baskets is the hardy golden form of common marjoram, *Origanum vulgare* 'Aureum'. It forms low spreading hummocks of soft green-gold, and the flavour is excellent. Sweet marjoram *Origanum majorana*, as the name suggests, has a sweeter flavour (and aroma), but isn't reliably hardy, so is best grown as an annual.

❀ MINT

Rapidly increasing from underground runners, mint is far too vigorous to be a long-term resident in a large basket or box, but it's well worth including in a 'summer only' planting. There are some very attractive forms, like yellow-variegated gingermint and the large, white-splashed leaves of variegated applemint. But the plain form of applemint, and green-leaved spearmint, have the finest flavour. It is easiest to care for in shade because it needs to be kept moist through any dry weather.

Chives

HERBS

❊ PARSLEY

We're not great fans of curled parsley – the flavour is a little acrid, and the texture is dry and crunchy, but flat-leaved French parsley is juicy and delicious; invaluable for both salads and cooked dishes. Buy young plants in spring, or sow it fresh each year. Warmth and a moist compost will ensure good germination. Grow in sun or partial shade, water well in dry weather, and remove any flowers that appear.

❊ ROSEMARY

Young rosemary plants are perfect for a hot, sunny window box, where their spires of blue-green, aromatic needles make a good backdrop for other plants. The flowers are pretty, too, especially if you go for a named form like bright blue 'Sissinghurst Blue'. Being evergreen perennials, they make good year-round residents, though the lease will probably run out after three or four years when they become rather woody and straggly. To keep them neat in the interim, trim them by up to half each spring. They will struggle in winter unless kept in a very sheltered position.

Variegated sage topping a basket.

Flat–leaved French parsley

❊ SAGE

Wonderfully pungent perennial evergreens for, again, a hot, sunny window box, forming neatly clothed domes. Instead of the plain grey-green, look out for the dusky purple sages, or for those with gold variegation – 'Kew Gold' is a beauty, with almost entirely yellow leaves, and just a few touches of green. All the sages (with the exception of pretty 'Tricolor') are completely hardy, but they share rosemary's tendency to woodiness, so are best replaced with fresh plants after a few years. Trim back in spring.

❊ THYME

A herb that's good for both window boxes and hanging baskets, forming low hummocks of tiny leaves and attractive summer flowers. Thymes make excellent edge-breakers for boxes, but are particularly effective in baskets, especially where a whole basket can be devoted to this fascinating group of plants. Here you can exploit the many foliage colours by weaving them together to create a tapestry effect, from lightest to darkest green, through silver-variegated to greeny yellows and glowing gold. Doubly lovely in summer when the flowers appear, adding a haze of pinks, mauves and magentas, crowded with happy bees. This is a basket that will also give great pleasure in winter, since thymes are evergreen and can be kept neat with a trim back after flowering. Thymes are great sun-lovers, and should be allowed to dry out between waterings.

FRUIT AND VEGETABLES

✤ AUBERGINES

If you've a sun-soaked window box in a sheltered position, then it's perfectly possible to grow a good crop of aubergines. Normal-sized plants would be a little too large, but you could try mini aubergines such as 'Bambino'. The plant grows to no more than 30cm/1ft high, producing clusters of 2.5cm/1in fruits which are delicious baked whole. Germinate in an airing cupboard or heated propagator in late winter or early spring, pot on, and plant out after all danger of frost has passed.

✤ BEETROOT

Beetroot is simplicity itself to grow from seed, and there are several baby varieties like 'Detroit 2 Little Ball' that reach no more than golf ball size, and the deep green leaves and red stems make a good contrast with other window box edibles. Sow *in situ*, from mid-spring to the end of summer, thinning to 5cm/2in apart when the seedlings emerge, to give them room to grow.

✤ CARROTS

Carrots are very fussy about soil – if it's heavy, or there's a hint of a stone, they grow forked and crooked. However, if you put them in a decent compost, they flourish. Stump-rooted varieties are ideal, but if it's the traditional shape you're after, go for 'Suko', a finger carrot growing to no more than 7.5cm/3in. Sow *in situ* from mid spring to midsummer, thinning to 2.5cm/1in apart to prevent overcrowding.

✤ FRENCH BEANS

Freshly-picked French beans have a superb flavour, so try to squeeze in

Stump-rooted carrot 'Parmex'.

one or two plants – they're rarely more than 30cm/1ft or so tall, so will fit in most window boxes very nicely. Choose a variety like 'Vilbel' or 'Aramis' (both exceedingly tasty), and pick regularly to keep them cropping. Sow in an airing cupboard or heated propagator in early spring and plant them in your box in late spring, or sow direct into the window box in mid spring.

✤ LETTUCE

A wonderful salad vegetable for all but south-facing window boxes; in a hot spot, they're prone to 'bolting' – sending up flowerheads and then dying. 'Little Gem' is the smallest of the cos lettuces, and very sweet, and the Iceberg 'Mini Green' is also superb – no bigger than an orange and packed with flavour, quite unlike the insipid Iceberg you usually get from the greengrocer. Loose-leaf lettuces are useful, too, not least because you can harvest just a few leaves at a time, and they can be very ornamental – 'New Red Fire', for instance, is spectacular, with compact, heavily frilled heads in darkest red. Sow *in situ* between mid spring and midsummer, thinning (since sizes vary somewhat), according to the packet instructions.

✤ PEPPERS

Sweet peppers need much the same conditions as aubergines and, again, there are plenty of miniature varieties, including 'Jingle Bells', 'Minibelle' and 'Redskin'. These produce a good crop of small fruits to no more than 4cm/1½in across, ripening from green to red. Germinate in an airing cupboard or heated propagator in early spring, pot on and plant out after the threat of frost has passed.

✤ RADISH

Radish is the all-time easy crop to grow, takes up very little space, and can be ready in under six weeks – ideal for sowing between young plants of other crops such as lettuces. Cylindrical

Radish 'Caravello'

'French Breakfast' is probably the best known, but the small globe types are very pretty in a salad, and colours range from cheery red through to pink and white. Sow in situ from early spring onwards, thinning to 2.5cm/1in apart.

❀ SPRING ONIONS
Being tall and slim, spring onions take up a minimum of space, so are ideal for window boxes. 'White Lisbon' is a tried and tested old favourite, with nicely plump bulbs and plenty of succulent green leaves for salads and stir fries. Sow *in situ* from early spring onwards, thinning to 2.5cm/1in apart and harvest when young. Keep well watered in dry weather.

Tomato 'Tumbler'

Strawberry 'Bounty'

❀ STRAWBERRIES
One of the most desirable of all fruits, and perfect for both window boxes and hanging baskets, where plants grow particularly well because they're safely out of the reach of soil-borne pests and diseases. For guaranteed good flavour, we like early 'Cambridge Vigour' and 'Honeoye', and mid-season 'Hapil' and 'Royal Sovereign'. Must have full sun.

❀ TOMATOES
There's just one tomato that will cope happily with life in a hanging basket or window box, and that's 'Tumbler'. It's naturally trailing, needs no pinching out, and produces dangling clusters of bright red, cherry-sized fruit with a good, sweet flavour. Germinate in an airing cupboard/germinator in early spring and plant out after the last frost. Keep evenly watered.

FRUIT AND VEGETABLES

Plant planner

If you're new to gardening, here's a quick-look guide to the plants you can use in your baskets, towers, pouches and window boxes. We've divided them up into two main categories – those for sun, and the heartening number of plants that will thrive in partial shade. We've also divided them into their different growth habits (upright, rounded and so on), so that you'll get the nice contrast of shapes that is so important, especially in window boxes.

Plants for sun

UPRIGHT HABIT

BEDDING
cineraria/senecio
cordyline
gazania
geranium (pelargonium) (some)
marguerite (argyanthemum)
marigold
tobacco plant (nicotiana)
osteospermum
polyanthus and primula

BULBS
chionodoxa
crocus
daffodil (narcissus)
dahlia
hyacinth
ipheion
iris reticulata
muscari
scilla
tulip

HERBS
chives
fennel
mint
rosemary

PERENNIALS
conifers (some)
heathers (some)

Osteospermum

Crocus

PLANTS FOR SUN

ROUNDED HABIT

BEDDING
begonia semperflorens
bellis
brachycome
busy lizzie (impatiens)
chrysanthemum
fuchsia
heliotrope
lobelia
nasturtium (some)
ornamental cabbage
pansy and viola
petunia

BULBS
begonia, tuberous

HERBS
basil
parsley
sage
thyme (some)

PERENNIALS
aucuba (laurel)
bay (*Laurus*)
box (*Buxus*)
conifers (some)
cotoneaster microphyllus
euonymus
hebe
heuchera
lonicera nitida

Lamium, viola and ajuga

pernettya
pieris (Forest flame)
santolina (Cotton lavender)
skimmia

MAT-FORMING HABIT

BEDDING
asteriscus
diascia
felicia
lamium
nemesia
portulaca
solenopsis (isotoma/laurentia)
verbena (some)

HERBS
marjoram
thyme (some)

PERENNIALS
ajuga
alpines (many)
gaultheria
heathers (some)

TRAILING HABIT

BEDDING
anagallis
bidens
centradenia
convolvulus
fuchsia (some)
geranium (some)
helichrysum
lobelia (some)
lotus
lysimachia
nasturtium (some)
nepeta (glechoma)
nolana
petunia (some)
plectranthus
polygonum
scaevola
sutura (bacopa)
verbena (some)

PERENNIALS
ivy (hedera)

Begonia semperflorens

Plants for partial shade

UPRIGHT HABIT

BEDDING
geranium
polyanthus and primula
tobacco plant (nicotiana)

BULBS
chionodoxa
daffodil (narcissus)
hyacinth
ipheion
scilla
snowdrop (galanthus)

HERBS
chives
mint

PERENNIALS
ferns (most)

ROUNDED HABIT

BEDDING
begonia
bellis
brachycome
busy lizzie (impatiens)
fuchsia
ornamental cabbage
pansy and viola

BULBS
begonia, tuberous

HERBS
parsley

PERENNIALS
aucuba
box (*Buxus*)
cotoneaster microphyllus
euonymus

heuchera
hosta
lonicera nitida
pieris (Forest flame)
skimmia

MAT-FORMING HABIT

BEDDING
lamium
mimulus (monkey flower)

PERENNIALS
ajuga
gaultheria

TRAILING HABIT

BEDDING
centradenia
fuchsia (some)
helichrysum 'Limelight'
lysimachia
nepeta (glechoma)
plectranthus
polygonum

PERENNIALS
ivy (hedera)

Geranium, fuchsia, tuberous begonia and helichrysum

Problem solving

Gardening in hanging baskets and window boxes is remarkably trouble-free so long as you follow our guidelines to choosing, planting and care. The plants are in good, comfortable compost, so are being pampered. The odd pest or disease might just creep in (like the dreaded vine weevil pictured left), but if you're vigilant, and deal with them promptly, they're unlikely to do any lasting damage.

PESTS

PESTS

GREENFLY AND BLACKFLY

By far the commonest of pests, these sap-sucking insects are bad news because they weaken and distort plant growth, and can transmit viruses from one plant to another. Vigilance is by far the best control – once you spot a little colony, it can be disposed of simply by squashing them between your fingers (but don't squeeze so hard that you crush the plant). The squeamish may like to use a tissue.

For more serious infestations, use an organic control such as soap-based Safer's Insecticide. If you opt for a chemical spray, try to use one like Miracle Garden Care Rapid which does minimal harm to beneficial insects. When you do spray, be thorough; don't forget the underside of leaves which seem to be a favourite spot for egg-laying and should be checked regularly.

LEAF MINERS

These are tiny insects that tunnel into leaf tissue, leaving a tell-tale scribble of white as the damaged tissue dies. Chrysanthemums are especially susceptible. Chemical sprays based on malathion are available, but in our experience it's much simpler just to pick off and destroy affected leaves as you spot them. The insects do little overall damage so unless you're growing for exhibition, spraying is overkill.

Greenfly come in all shades from green to brown.

The tunnelling leaf miner disfigures leaves.

P E S T S

Whitefly can be difficult to eradicate.

RED SPIDER MITE

You'll need a magnifying glass if you want to see this tiny spider, but the signs of its presence are a very fine, irregular webbing and a pinprick, pale mottling on the leaves. They're lovers of hot, dry spots, so the easiest way to control them is to change the conditions – there's nothing much you can do about the heat, but they'll loathe it if you keep your plants nicely moist, and mist over the leaves now and again. They'll squelch away in search of pastures new.

SLUGS AND SNAILS

We tend to think of slugs and snails as ground-dwellers, but they're remarkably athletic – a point brought home when one of us spotted a snail on the outside of a window 3m/10ft above the ground.

So they might well invade your window box or even, with a bit of ingenuity and a following wind, your hanging basket. The damage they do is pretty obvious – tattered and holed leaves, sometimes reduced to a skeleton, and a tell-tale trail of silvery slime.

The simplest way of getting rid of them is to scatter a few slug pellets in the box or basket, or if you're an organic gardener, to simply pick them off – dusk is the best time to spot them, especially on a damp evening. There is also a biological control containing microscopic, death-dealing eelworms, but it's only effective against slugs.

VINE WEEVIL

The scourge of the container gardener. The adult stage is a small, slow-moving beetle, grey-brown with a light dusting of gold speckles. They're quite capable of rambling up walls, and when they've nibbled a few notches out of the edges of your leaves, they burrow down to lay eggs. The resultant larvae (fat, off-white with a brown head, up to 13mm/½in long) can wreak considerable havoc. Hidden away in the compost, they feast on the roots of your precious plants, and the first sign of their presence is a wilting, followed by a total, and fatal, collapse.

If you do get an infestation, it's important (if soul-destroying) to dismantle the whole container. Shake as much soil from the plants as possible, checking through the rootball for any remaining larvae, then replant in fresh compost. To control them in future, squash the adults on sight, and always check the compost of newly bought plants for signs of the grubs (commercial growers are extremely careful, but a few will inevitably slip through). If they're a major pest in your container plantings, the very best way of dealing with the problem is to use a biological control (eelworms again), watered onto the soil in spring or late summer; it really is very effective.

WHITEFLY

These are the small, white insects that fly up in clouds when plants are disturbed. In our experience they do no major damage to the plants, but their sticky, 'honeydew' droppings can encourage the growth of unsightly sooty mould. To control them, use a soap-based organic insecticide, or a chemical insecticide containing pirimicarb – several applications will be necessary, and they're almost impossible to eliminate entirely.

DISEASES

POWDERY MILDEW

This is one of the commonest diseases that affects many container plants, a fungus that gets a grip in hot, dry weather, especially if you're not watering as often as you should. Leaves are coated in a fine, white powder, and new shoots can be badly affected, with stunted, distorted growth. To control it, remove and destroy all affected material (sometimes whole plants, sadly), and keep containers well watered. If the attack is severe, spray with Bordeaux mixture (organic) or Bio Dithane 945 (chemical).

DOWNY MILDEW

Superficially, this is similar to powdery mildew, but it coats the undersides of leaves, with a yellowing of the upper surfaces. It's commonest after a prolonged wet spell, particularly in very dense plantings. Destroy all affected material, and check the drainage holes in window boxes to make sure they're not clogged up. Spray severe attacks with Phostrogen Safer's Liquid Fungicide (organic) or Bio Supercarb (chemical).

ROTS

Fortunately, rots are pretty rare. Stems and leaves turn slimy, and there's usually a fluffy, grey/brown mould in evidence. Almost without exception, rots are caused by poor drainage together with overwatering, and spring bulbs, quietly growing away unseen through most of the winter, are the most susceptible. So always make sure that window boxes, in particular, have very sharp drainage, and don't

Powdery mildew can spread rapidly in hot, dry weather.

TIPS

✔ *Cleanliness is a great ally in the war against diseases so always give window boxes and hanging baskets a thorough clean-out between plantings.*

✔ *Whenever you're deadheading or watering, just check your plants over for the first sign of any pests or diseases. If you catch them at an early stage, they're much easier to eradicate and little harm will have been done.*

✔ *Rusts (brown or orange spots on leaves) can seriously weaken plant growth, but they are rare on most container plants. Geraniums, however, can be susceptible, especially after a wet spell, so if you notice anything, remove and destroy the affected leaves. It is the 'zonal' geraniums (the bushy varieties with rounded, scalloped leaves) that are at risk – the trailing ivy-leafed forms, happily, are not affected.*

overwater them in cool, damp weather. If the rot isn't too far advanced, the plant can be saved by removing affected material, but in the case of severe rot, destroy the entire plant.

DISEASES

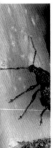

HOLIDAY CARE

As we've stressed, hanging baskets and window boxes need regular watering, feeding and dead-heading through summer if they're to look their very best. So what do you do when holiday time comes around?

The simplest solution is to find a kindly neighbour who will do the watering for you (and the feeding if your absence is longer than two weeks). But don't impose the chore of dead-heading on them – a couple of weeks' neglect in this department won't do lasting harm. Just leave the watering can and feed handy, send them a postcard, and bring them back a nice present.

If you've fallen out with all the neighbours, or they're off on holiday at the same time, sterner measures are called for. If you're only going away for a week or so, move hanging baskets to a cool and shady position and water them thoroughly just before you leave. Smaller window boxes, too, can be given this treatment.

For a longer absence, the best option is to move containers to a shady position and, in addition, rig up a rudimentary watering system. First, stand a large bucket or bin on bricks and fill it with water, to create a reservoir. Then cluster the containers around it and give each one an umbilical cord to the water supply using thin strips of capillary matting cut from a roll. These should be long enough to reach from the bottom of the reservoir to the container, where they are firmly tucked into the compost. Check that the system is working by putting it in place a few days before your holiday – really thirsty containers may need more than one strip of matting.

The ultimate solution, though, especially with larger window boxes

A drip feed watering system.

that are difficult to lift, is to install a drip feed watering system. This is a series of drip heads and plastic tubing connected to a hose, some with a master unit that filters the water and reduces the pressure to create a gentle (and adjustable) drip.

It certainly solves the watering problem, whether you're on holiday or not, but it can take quite some ingenuity to hide the tubing neatly away – in our experience, securing it with black cable clips makes a good, discreet job of it.

BETTER SAFE THAN SORRY

Window boxes, which are generally secured into position, are pretty safe from theft, but it has become quite common to read of thieves making off with hanging baskets – and as often as not, selling them to an unsuspecting householder just round the corner.

For the most part though, these are opportunists, making a quick raid by unhooking the basket, and an even quicker getaway. They're highly unlikely to be armed with bolt cutters, so securing the basket to the bracket is an excellent deterrent. This could be something as simple as attaching the basket to the bracket with strong wire – few thieves will hang around in broad daylight patiently undoing it. You can also buy security kits consisting of a basket and bracket that are connected by a special padlock, and Babyllon bowls have a bowl lock as an optional extra.

Index

GARDEN NOTES